REAL

THE INSIDE OUT GUIDE TO BEING YOURSELF

CLARE DIMOND

By Garret Kramer,
author of *Stillpower* and *The Path of No Resistance*

Seldom are the encounters in life so pure and so perfect. Yet, this is exactly how I'd describe the moment when I first met my dear friend, Clare Dimond. I knew in an instant that I'd stumbled upon the most genuine of human beings. I also knew that both of our lives had been changed forever.

Clare was a participant in a workshop that I was conducting in London. That weekend, she didn't say much. But when she did speak, it was in such a real, fluent, and natural way that not only did the room fall silent, but it was obvious to me that I was listening to someone called to teach. To guide. To point others to the source of all suffering and, thus, to suffering's only cure. I saw in my new friend that rare combination of eloquence, grace, and no-nonsense. I saw someone called to write this book.

In *Real,* Clare presents age-old wisdom in her own fresh and unique way. This wisdom will challenge your beliefs; it will clash with the indoctrination of your upbringing; it will have you scratching your head. But it will also bring moving glimpses of freedom and relief. *Real* will subtly remind you that you can't be broken. That insecurity and weakness are just as normal as confidence and strength. Clare has written *Real* because she wants you to take a deep look at where your experiences—your feelings, sensations, perceptions, and emotions—are actually coming from, and what they are telling you.

Just one small suggestion as you work your way through this book: Take time to savour and appreciate the experience. If Clare has taught me anything, it's been to slow down a bit and relish the power of the paradigm that you're about to take in.

Real offers hope for our children and promise for the future of mankind. It proves that the circumstances of your life are not limiting and that everything you experience comes from within. Read Clare's words and reflect on their meaning. I'm sure that like me when I finished the final chapter, you'll realize that, regardless of your current mood or feeling state, you are whole, capable, and loved—always and forever.

I wish you good luck.

Garret Kramer

Morristown, New Jersey, USA

The one thing that the most productive, consistent, resilient, and loving human beings
do NOT possess is an intense belief in themselves.
Garret Kramer

And in this game of life, we all search for ourselves.
When I say selves, I mean 'inner selves', the thing that created the life in the first place.
Now consciously, most of us are not aware of this.
But if you're searching for happiness; if you're searching for tranquility;
if you're searching just to have a nice, peaceful, loving, understanding life...
in actual fact, you are searching for your inner self.
Sydney Banks

THE DISRUPTION

Only to the extent that we expose ourselves over and over to annihilation can that which is indestructible in us be found.
Pema Chödrön

If this book does its job, it will start to shake the precarious house of cards that is your idea of who you are.

If it succeeds, a lifetime's work of weaving belief into belief will unravel until your thoughts about yourself become a pile of loose threads.

This might not be comfortable.

It sounds like the opposite of what we want a book to do. We read books about self-esteem and self-confidence. We want books that reinforce our self-belief. We want books that build us up. The last thing we want is for our sense of self to be shaken or unravelled.

You might already be thinking / saying / shouting 'Back off, Clare. Who I am is who I am! Don't mess with that.'

Please stay with the book. I promise, everything you have ever been looking for comes from seeing more clearly who you really are and who you cannot possibly be.

We have an identity, an idea of something that we think we are. It looks solid and true. This identity tells us what we can and can't do. It tells us what upsets and scares us. It tells us what makes us angry. It tells us who loves and hates us. It tells us our limits and what we are good at. It seems to draw people in or create employment or inspire love. It seems to give us something stable to cling on to.

And, if you are like me, then you might sometimes feel that something is missing.

You might sometimes feel that other people have life more sorted than you.

You might feel that you need to secure who you are through your career or relationships.

You might have been trying to 'be someone', to feel better about who you are.

You might have taken jobs or said or done things, that deep down you didn't want to, in order to be secure, respected or loved or successful.

You might have thoughts that say you are wrong or inadequate or incapable. You might do things to try to blank out those thoughts.

A lot of effort. A lot of building up. A lot of blanking out. And all of it in order to secure a self that we think has to be preserved and defended.

And that is about to end. And that can be uncomfortable.

Which might be why, in talks I have given, occasionally someone has started to cry. (I realise that is not the best advert for my talks...) One dear friend said through her tears, "But if I am not who I think I am, who am I? Not knowing who I am is terrifying to me."

And a client said to me, "If I am not my identity, then how will I know what to do? Will I end up doing nothing at all?"

Another client said, 'Who will I be if I'm not what I think? What will guide my decisions?'

The fear is that if we no longer believe the thoughts telling us who we are then we will disappear. As though the thoughts were somehow making us real, were fixing us in the earth, giving us a place.

The fear is that if we no longer believe the voice telling us what we should or should not be doing, we will have no motivation to do anything. We will sink into oblivion on a tapestry yoga cushion.

The fear is that without our beliefs about who we are, without an idea of a personality or identity, we will be empty, vacuous, left wanting, doing nothing.

THE OPPOSITE IS TRUE.

When we glimpse the truth of who we are beneath the stories, whatever remains is more real, not less. It is more engaged and more loving and more passionate. We realise we (whatever that 'we' is) are more than we could ever have thought possible.

Way, way more.

The fear of losing our created self to get closer to what lies beneath it is logical. Pema Chödrön, the American Tibetan Buddhist and author, said, "Fear is a natural reaction to moving closer to the truth".

So why would we move closer?

Because our idea of a self isn't a true self. Our idea of who we are is a compilation of changing thoughts and beliefs. Who we think we are is not who we are, never was and never will be.

Deep down, we know this. We know that everything we think about who we are can flip to the opposite thought in a heartbeat. One minute, we think we are a loser. The next minute, we think we are doing OK. One moment, we think we are kind. The next moment, we believe we are nasty. One moment it looks like people love and respect us. The next we seem like an outcast.

Our idea of self is unstable, insecure, volatile and untrue.

We can go a step further in these bold assertions…

What we think about ourselves and the world is the only cause of any problem we ever have.

This false idea of who we are is the source of every limit and every burden, all insecurity and anxiety, every frustration and disappointment, all lies and deception, every conflict and every suffering.

Sometimes these beliefs about who we are and who we should be seem overwhelming. That critical voice going through our head can seem unbearable. Many of us resort to extreme measures to have a moment's respite.

With each insight into the creative power of thought, we start to see the truth about ourselves.

A truth that is beyond anything we have ever experienced in our life.

A truth beyond what we ever thought possible.

WHO ARE YOU?

I want you to be everything that's you,
deep at the centre of your being.
Confucius

The energy of the mind is the essence of life.
Aristotle

Our life is what our thoughts make it.
Marcus Aurelius

Each one has to find his peace from within.
Mahatma Gandhi

In 1973, Sydney Banks, a welder living in Salt Spring Island, had a profound insight. He realised that we live in a projected, ever-changing reality and that there is a deeper constancy underneath the illusion of this projection.

This realisation was nothing new. Philosophers, gurus, enlightened leaders, scientists and writers (including those quoted above and throughout this book) have long had the same insight. It is as old as our ability to recognise that we think.

What Syd Banks brought was simplicity.

He articulated this insight as the three principles of Thought, Consciousness and Mind.

In three words, he summed up the whole breadth of our experience.

Thought: our entire experience is a momentary 'reality' created in thought. It shifts and changes as the energy of thought ebbs and flows.

Consciousness: the awareness of thinking. The space in which all of 'reality' is conceived.

Mind: the universal intelligence that gives life to all things, that brings about existence.

This articulation is sometimes known as 'The Three Principles' or 'The Inside Out Understanding'. The transformation that results from seeing this is breathtaking.

In 2012 I read 'The Inside Out Revolution' by Michael Neill. It was the first time I had heard of Sydney Banks. Despite having spent decades studying human development, it was the first time I had heard experience described with such simplicity. It was the first time I saw genuine transformation in myself and others.

I realised that everything is being created through momentary, transient thought. Everything I think about who I am and how the world is and how I had to be and what I had to do to be loved or appreciated is all created in thought. All of it is changing.

As these beliefs began to unravel, there was more lightness, more freedom. The exhaustion disappeared. Busyness of head disappeared. Stress disappeared.

This is why Jamie Smart, bestselling author of 'Clarity' and 'Results', calls this understanding 'subtractive psychology'.

It is seeing through the stuff that cannot be true, that no longer seems relevant.

The first part of this book looks at everything that is not true. It looks at what evolves and transforms and which cannot be who we are. This is true subtractive psychology. Seeing through the transient. Understanding the ever-changing and ephemeral. It is the realisation of what we are not.

Seeing through all the things that we are not leaves us with one big question: who are we?

The second half of the book explores what remains when our idea of self looks less fixed. It explores what is constant, what is always there regardless of transient thought and belief. By looking for the constant and unchanging we get closer to the truth of who we are.

And it is universal truth. There is no one that this truth doesn't apply to.

To be human and alive is to be this constancy.

There are no exceptions.

It is the realisation of what we are.

PART 1: YOU ARE NOT

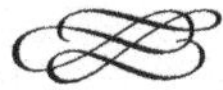

In ignorance, I am something;
In understanding, I am nothing;
In love, I am everything.
Rupert Spira

*L*et's start with who you are not.

There is so much that we think defines us that does not even come close.

And when we believe all the things we are not, then we miss all the things that we are.

If you are like I was for decades, you might worry about your weaknesses, your past or future. You might think you should be more like someone else. You might strive to be better, stronger, more able. You might sometimes feel defeated, incapable. You might compare yourself and judge.

Have you done psychological tests that conclude you are a plant or a red hat or an ENTJ? Are you an introvert or extrovert?

Do you have a good idea of your limits and your strengths? Do you know the things you should stick to?

Are you successful enough? Are you interesting? Do people like you? Do you ever think you should be different? Do you ever wish you were more important and more respected or less anxious.

All of this, every test given with such good intention, every assessment, each category of who we are is pointing in the direction of a made-up idea that only exists for as long as it is believed.

The truth is that it is impossible to define you.

There is no measure that can put a frame around you and say 'this' but not 'this'.

Your thoughts alone create your experience of who you are, moment by moment.

My thoughts alone create my experience of who you are, moment by moment.

Your experience of you and my experience of you changes all the time.

In the moment that this experience is believed, that seems to be who you are.

But what if we saw through it?

What if we realised that, 24 hours a day, thought is flowing through our minds. Some of that thought we will notice, believe, act on and, from that, an apparent reality is created.

When we see that the content of thought is fluid, ever-changing and transient, it has far less validity or gravitas.

The purpose of this first section is to discover how our lives, our idea of self, are held in thought. Because when we see this, we start to see what we are beyond the changing content of our thinking.

There might well be moments when everything that is said here looks wrong or impossible. It might look as though it goes against everything you have believed your entire life.

My only request in these moments is that you continue reading, continue exploring. Something might resonate with what you know, deep down, to be true. This book is here to help you explore your own inner knowledge, your own integrity and truth. It doesn't matter what anyone else thinks or says.

Take your time with it and notice how you are able to simply be. How you are able to glimpse the infinite creative capacity of thought. To notice that you have access to a deep inner knowing of what to do. How you are able to notice your ability to notice.

This is the end of positive thinking, self-improvement, will power and working on ourselves. It is the end of the search for self-esteem and self-confidence. It it is the end of the attempt to 'be someone'. None of that is relevant anymore.

Because no matter how hard we try to secure ourselves and our lives, a single thought can change the whole set up from one moment to the next.

It all looks so real. Yet all it is is transient thought. A reflection of a state of mind. Nothing more than that. Our entire perception of who we are is temporary.

If you think you know who you are, you are surely mistaken.

If you know deep down that you have no idea of who you

are, of what is guiding and powering you, then you are getting closer to the truth.

It is so easy to forget because it all looks so real. All we can do is remind ourselves of the truth of who we are, of who other people are, of how the world is.

This book is designed as a series of reminders to do just that. We're starting with the enormous thought-created realm of what you are not.

YOU ARE NOT.

YOU ARE NOT YOUR THOUGHTS

Understanding the nature of thought frees us from the illusion of our thinking.
Michael Neill, The Space Within

I am a yoga teacher as well as a coach. Before I realised the nature of thought I used to tell my students to empty their minds. I told them to get rid of thoughts and to sit there in peace.

What a ridiculous thing to tell someone.

Talk about messing with people's heads.

It is impossible to empty our minds of thought. Thoughts appear. Out of nowhere. To try not to think is to think even more. Try it.

"I mustn't think of anything. I mustn't think of anything. I mustn't... Hold on. Does thinking 'I mustn't think of anything' count as thinking...? What will I have for dinner? Oh shit. I'm thinking about dinner. That's definitely thinking. I'm such a loser. I can't even do this for 30 seconds. No wonder my life is such a disaster…"

We blame ourselves for not being able to empty our mind but it is an impossible task. It is as out of our control as the clouds in the sky.

It is the same with positive thinking. We tell people to notice a negative thought and replace it with a thought that is happier.

Again, talk about messing with people's heads.

"Right. I'm only going to think positive thoughts. I'm going to start with thoughts about… my boss. She is a really nice person. She is a really nice person. She is a really ni… Well… she let me take the rap for something that was actually her fault. And then she was all smarmy with the CEO. She doesn't care about me. She wants me out. She's a real bitch. I hate her." Uh oh.

It is impossible to change the nature or the content of thought. It is impossible to control, filter or select thoughts. Next time you are in a real funk, fed up with life, try forcing yourself to think that everything is great. It doesn't work. We get even more pissed off about the world and ourselves.

There is no control over the timing, content, tone, frequency of the thoughts that pass through.

'Thanks Clare,' you might be thinking now, in an inner voice laden with sarcasm. 'Great! So where do I go from here? I'm stuck with all this stuff am I?'

It might seem that because we cannot change our thoughts, then we *are* our thoughts.

It might seem that we are doomed to live out the life and character that our thoughts dictate.

This is like saying that the clouds are the sun. It is like saying the boats on the river are the river or the ants marching along the branch are the branch.

Thoughts flow through the mind. Clouds move across the sun. Boats float downstream. Ants scurry along a branch.

The thoughts are not who we are. The clouds are not the sun. The boats are not the river. The ants are not the branch.

The thoughts (or the clouds, boats and ants for that matter) don't say anything about us. We don't even know where thoughts come from. Warren Ellis, the social commentator, asked the provocative question, "If you believe that your thoughts originate inside your brain, do you also believe that television shows are made inside your television set?'

Sometimes, though, the thoughts are believed. They are taken seriously. They momentarily become 'reality'.

Sometimes this thought-created reality is exhausting. Sometimes we believe that we are worthless or that the world is out to get us or that we do not deserve to thrive. When we believe this 'reality' we suffer.

No wonder we numb ourselves through drugs, alcohol, shopping, tv, games, sex, whatever. This works until whatever it is wears off and we are right back in the exhaustion and suffering. This is the origin of addiction. Temporary relief from a painful mind.

And there is a miracle way to break the circle forever.

This miracle lies in the realisation that experience is created in thought.

It lies in the realisation that there is no point trying to 'fix' thought because that is futile and impossible. There is nothing to fix. Thought comes and goes, ebbs and flows. Sometimes self-congratulatory, sometimes full of self blame. Sometimes at ease, sometimes anxious. Sometimes happy, sometimes depressed.

There is nothing to investigate or to believe or not believe or to fix or control. It is simply energy floating through our mind. We don't need to do anything about it.

The experience of thought is a permanent feature of the conscious human mind. The ability to think is part of who we are.

The actual thoughts themselves, their content, form, structure, frequency are nothing to do with who we are or how well we are doing or what sort of person we are.

You are not your thoughts.

YOU ARE NOT WHO YOU THINK YOU ARE

The beginning of freedom is the realisation that you are not 'the thinker'. The moment you start watching the thinker, a higher level of consciousness becomes activated.
You then begin to realise that there is a vast realm of intelligence beyond thought, that thought is only a tiny aspect of that intelligence.
You also realise that all the things that truly matter — beauty, love, creativity, joy, inner peace —
arise from beyond the mind. You begin to awaken.
Eckhart Tolle

Thought is ever-changing. It ebbs and flows as our mental energy ebbs and flows. Like the tide flowing in and out. A reality is created according to this ever-changing energy.

OUT OF OUR LOW STATE OF MIND, it looks like people are annoying, out to get us, unhelpful.

OUT OF OUR LOW STATE OF MIND, it looks like circumstances are difficult and tedious.

OUT OF OUR HIGHER STATE OF MIND, it looks like people love us and want to help us.

OUT OF OUR HIGHER STATE OF MIND it looks like circumstances are fun, full of potential and possibility.

There are no objective, fixed and static people and circumstances out there. There is an experience that changes as our mental energy changes.

This tends to be what people see more clearly when they start exploring the inside-out nature of reality. They can see that, one moment, they are really fed up with their kids or the partner or their colleagues. And the next moment, they enjoy their company. It is not so hard to see that it is not the kids, partner or colleagues changing.

What is harder to see is that our entire idea of who we are is also created out of the changing energy that gives rise to thought.

OUT OF OUR LOW STATE OF MIND, it looks like there is a self that is a failure or a loser, that deserves blame.

OUT OF OUR HIGHER STATE OF MIND, it looks like there is a self that is doing pretty well, that has life sorted.

THERE ARE NO OTHER PEOPLE THAT EXIST INDEPENDENTLY OF THOUGHT. There are creations of a state of mind.

THERE ARE NO CIRCUMSTANCES THAT EXIST INDEPENDENTLY OF THOUGHT. There are creations of a state of mind.

THERE IS NO INDIVIDUAL SELF THAT EXISTS INDEPENDENTLY OF THOUGHT. There is only ever a creation of a state of mind.

This is the biggest game changer of all time. Writing it now, my hands are shaking and I have butterflies in my stomach. There is no self. There is an idea of a self, produced from a state of mind. But everything we think about that self is simply thought believed in that moment.

We are not our thoughts. And we are not who we think we are.

Every single thing we think about ourselves can change. Not only can it change, it can turn into the direct opposite. Some beliefs may hang around for longer. Yet, they too disappear as we see that they also come and go with the energy of mind.

YOU ARE NOT WHO YOU THINK YOU ARE.

YOU ARE NOT YOUR BELIEFS

Belief is the death of intelligence
Robert Anton Winston

In her book *Mind Over Medicine*, American doctor Lissi Rankin cites a study in San Diego which examined the death records of almost 30,000 Chinese-Americans and compared them to the records of over 400,000 randomly selected white people.

The study found that 'Chinese-Americans but not whites, die significantly earlier (by as much as five years) if they have a combination of disease and birth year which Chinese astrology and Chinese medicine consider ill-fated'.

The effect of placebos (positive effect despite no treatment) and nocebos (negative effect despite no treatment) is well documented.

Studies have shown that, when teachers are told that some children in the class are particularly bright, those children show greater improvement than the children who the teacher believed were less able.

Our beliefs govern life, health, relationships, impact, even the time of death.

We have beliefs about the world, about other people, about the weather, about what is right or wrong.

Our beliefs seem to form a core to us and to the world, a consistency. By definition, we don't see them as beliefs, we see them as true. And because they look true, they have immense power.

We have beliefs about who we are and all of this looks 100% accurate to us. Irrefutable. It has to because it is a belief.

Our beliefs create the reality we live and die in.

YET THEY ARE NOT WHO WE ARE.

They are not who we are because every single belief has the potential to change.

I am…

I am not…

I can…

I can't…

I will…

I won't…

I should…

I shouldn't…

All of it based on beliefs that can change in a heartbeat with new information.

With a new perspective, every single aspect of our identity and what we make it mean is up for grabs.

With fresh information, a new reality appears.

With greater understanding of how 'reality' is constructed, beliefs, even decades old, can disappear without trace. Just watch...

YOU ARE NOT YOUR BELIEFS.

YOU ARE NOT YOUR FEELINGS

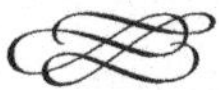

100% of our feeling is arising from THOUGHT in the moment
Jamie Smart

I sometimes give talks on the inside out understanding.

The simple fact that I am giving a talk is evidence of the freedom in seeing the power of thought to create feeling.

For decades, I had an abject fear of public speaking. Even the mention of a presentation at work made me feel sick and faint. I couldn't even ask a question in a meeting. I tried everything to get rid of that terrible anxiety. I went on courses. I tried deep breathing, relaxation techniques, hypnosis, rescue remedies, visualisation, affirmations, rehearsing, not rehearsing, the naked audience trick, standing up, sitting down, brandy… Nothing worked.

The more I tried to get rid of this fear the more of a thing it became. It became an Issue. A Phobia. A Problem. I had to

Deal With It. Find A Solution. And the more the capital letters appeared, the more impossible it became.

What I realise, as I understand more about how we experience life, is that fear can be terrible. It can be something that someone will try to avoid at all costs, just as I did.

Or it can be something we pay thousands of dollars to experience on an adventure holiday. Or something we want so much that we demand a refund if the latest horror film doesn't live up to the hype.

Awful or amazing. Devastating or desirable.

The only difference is whether we think we want it or not. Which means that apart from a belief about it, fear is neither positive or negative. As it is for fear, so it is for all our other feelings: anger, sadness, calm, joy, concern, anxiety, grief…

Wow.

A director I worked with once believed she was being authentic and true to herself when she brought every changing mood to the office.

Panicked and insecure, she would hassle her team.

Angry and defensive she would stamp around and shout down the phone.

Gloomy and low, she would hide herself away.

Happy and at ease, she would shower her team in praise and goodwill.

If she is her feelings, who is she? Angry? Nervous? Gloomy? Happy? These are just feelings she is experiencing according to mental energy in the moment. None of it gives any indication of anything other than her mental state.

The feelings do not indicate who she is. They do not indicate how well other people are performing. They do not indicate the state of the business or the economy. When she believes they do, that becomes her reality for the moment.

She is experiencing feelings in her physical body. Low energy or a fast beating heart or a squirming stomach - these are all physical events that we feel. Experiencing these, without labelling them or categorising them as good or bad takes us as close as we can to the reality of this body. We can acknowledge these sensations. No amount of ignoring or denying them will push them away. They are there, being felt.

Seeing this is a transformational shift in the direction of the truth of our experience.

When we don't want to feel something, we try to squash or override the physical sensations. At the same time, we don't question the thoughts that are creating those sensations.

I desperately tried to get rid of the physical. I did everything I could to still my shaking hands and squash the crazy butterflies in my stomach. These sensations were not acceptable to me.

Not for one moment, though, did I question the thoughts telling me I was a loser, that I shouldn't be afraid, that people would laugh at me, that I had to feel differently.

With greater understanding, we come into reality. Beliefs and thoughts are seen for what they are - transient and insubstantial. Physical sensations are acknowledged and unresisted.

I can give a talk and my hands can be shaking and my voice can tremble. I can blush and sweat and lose my words and dry up and fumble and stumble. The only way any of that is a problem is if I think it is. And even then, it's not a problem.

It is the resistance that creates the issue.

When I don't cling to or resist thoughts of how any experience is to be avoided or welcomed then I simply experience it, feelings and all.

None of it is who I am. All of it is simply experience, taking place in the moment. This realisation is freedom.

YOU ARE NOT YOUR FEELINGS.

Your habit is not "you" and it is not personal.
It is simply your brain doing what it does.
Amy Johnson

Clients sometimes come into my office and spread out their habits before me as if to say, "Here I am. Look at me. What a disaster I am. I drink too much wine in the evenings. I over-work. I can't keep a relationship. I want to go to the gym but I never get there. I eat pizzas and take-aways. I'm terrible with money. Sort me out please. Make me someone different."

None of this is who they are of course. How could the magnificence of the individual in front of me be reduced to what they eat or how often they work out?

Habits reflect our relationship with our understanding of who we are. No more no less.

If we believe the thinking going through our mind, and if it bothers us or causes us to suffer and we think we need to have more mental peace, the chances are we will have habits that try to control that thinking in some way.

If we believe that a certain behaviour is necessary for our well-being, that behaviour will be part of our life.

We might try to blank out self-criticism or anxiety with drink or drugs. We might use overwork or the tv to silence thoughts that say we are a failure. We might hoard or be reckless to quieten fears about the future. If we feel unloved or unworthy we might use relationships or sex to show how desirable we are.

But when we simply see the thinking for what it is, transient energy flowing through, we don't have to do anything to change it.

As Dr Amy Johnson, author of 'The Little Book of Big Change' and expert in releasing habits, says "Lifelong freedom comes from insight. From seeing life—yourself, your habits, and how the human mind works in a radically different way. Freedom comes from inside you through insight not from implementing behavioural tactics. When you see differently, you naturally do things differently."

When we don't need to change ourselves or the outside world to realise we are OK, our behaviour falls into line with that clarity. Patterns of behaviour that have been with us for decades can disappear the moment we see the nature of who we are more truthfully.

YOU ARE NOT YOUR HABITS.

YOU ARE NOT DEFINED BY SURROUNDINGS

The mind is its own place and, in itself,
can make a hell of heaven, a heaven of hell.
John Milton, Paradise Lost

My husband and I were camping in Canada one year. I woke up one morning, as the cold dawn light pierced the tent. I had had a dismal night worrying about bears. There was frost on the outside of my sleeping bag. I had jet lag and a headache. I felt awful, freezing, aching, stiff. We'll find a hotel I thought. James isn't going to want to stay here any longer.

I crawled out of the tent to get his view on how we could salvage this disaster of a holiday.

There he was, in his favourite woolly hat and fleece. He was sitting on a tree stump, next to the camp stove, holding a steaming cup of tea. He was gazing out on the landscape with the expression of the purest, brightest joy and contentment I had ever seen. Shit, I thought.

One set of surroundings: a tent, the cold, Canada, bears. Two opposite experiences. It cannot be the surroundings that are causing the feelings. It was the mental energy of James and the mental energy of me. And both can change. As my state of mind changed I had a great time. As his state of mind changed he had moments of frustration and lowness. And this changed over and over again. Out of our control.

How we perceive our surroundings is only ever a reflection of our state of mind in the moment. We can have a terrible or wonderful time or anything else in a fifteen bed mansion. We can have a terrible or wonderful time or anything else in a hostel.

Surroundings are creations in consciousness.

What happens though is that we forget this.

We forget that experience of place is simply thought in the moment. We believe that what we see out there, where we live, where we work, where we holiday say something about who we are.

We can look at our bed in the five star hotel and think 'I've made it!' or 'I'm a loser.'

We can look at our sleeping bag in the off-grid trailer and think 'I've made it!' or 'I'm a loser.'

Energy in the moment creates what we see. It is always that way round. We believe our surroundings tell us something about how we are doing in life.

We believe they tell us about who we are.

They don't.

YOU ARE NOT DEFINED BY YOUR SURROUNDINGS.

YOU ARE NOT YOUR PAST

It is impossible to say a thing exactly the way it was, because what you say can never be exact, you always have to leave something out, there are too many parts, sides, crosscurrents, nuances; too many gestures, which could mean this or that, too many shapes, which can never be fully described, too many flavours in the air or on the tongue, half colours, too many.
Margaret Atwood, *The Handmaid's Tale*

My clients will sometimes say things like 'I was bullied in school so I am shy and nervous.'

Or: 'My Dad left us when I was young so I will never fully trust anyone'.

Or 'My parents used to fight about money so now I don't like anything to do with it'.

The past often has such a starring role in our lives. We can believe that it dictates the way we react to things in the world, that it has created the person we believe ourselves to be.

The past seems like some fixed, objective truth. A powerful influence that has our present and future in its iron jaw. This is how it was, therefore this is how I am and this is how I will be. And there seems no way round this. It seems so real and the implications seem so inevitable.

But hold on.

Everything we are experiencing right now is 100% created through thought. From the inside out, everything around us appears. We only ever experience thought in the moment. This is true now. It is true in every moment of our lives.

I can only ever remember the past from this moment right now in the present. My memories—their content, tone, form, and presence—are created according to my state of mind in the moment.

In a low state of mind, it seems there must be reasons for that low state. The mind creates a story to explain it.

In a higher state of mind, it seems there must be reasons for that high state of mind. The mind creates a story to explain it.

We are not *responding* to reality because there is no reality. Reality is a creation emerging through mental energy. What appears as a memory, is only ever a sign of my current state. Nothing else.

Often my clients when they first come to see me want to tell me the details of their past. It is useful as an indication of the state of mind they are in right there in my room.

What they remember and the significance they give a memory will change. These memories have no bearing on what they are capable of or who they are or who they will be in five minutes time.

I will give you a personal example, if I may.

My father died of leukaemia when I was ten.

Sometimes I am sad and I miss him. Sometimes I know he is here with me.

Sometimes I wish my children could have known him. Sometimes I think of how my Mum would not have met her beautiful partner of 30 years if he had not died.

Sometimes I think of how surviving that has made all of us so strong. Sometimes I think of how damaged we were by his death.

Sometimes I think the world is cruel for that to happen. Sometimes I think the world is kind and how we are never asked to handle more than we can cope with.

What is the truth in all of that?

He died.

How I see the meaning of his death (and, in fact, the meaning of death as a concept), the implications of it, the effect on me is thought in the moment. Good or bad. Sad or happy. Positive or negative. It can be anything.

All of it will change from moment to moment. None of it is fixed.

To investigate the impact of my father's death would send me and any poor therapist down a rabbit warren. We would get lost in tunnels that appear and collapse from one moment to the next as energy changes.

You cannot be your past. It is just not possible. It cannot dictate who you are because it has no power to do that. You can only ever experience beliefs and thoughts in any one moment. And the more you see this, the clearer it is that those beliefs and thoughts do not define you in any way.

Our memories do not reflect the reality of the past because reality is only ever a creation from within from moment to moment.

You are not your past. You can never be your past. It has no objective or truthful meaning. It is nothing that will not change from one moment to the next.

You are not your past.

YOU ARE NOT IN CONTROL

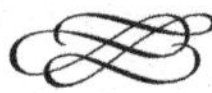

Trying to assume personal control—over anything—is simply not possible. What a relief.
Garret Kramer

Imagine that you are driving and you bump another car. The other driver gets out of the car in full rage. You have no control over what this driver will do. She could do anything.

You also have no control over the thoughts that appear in your mind at that moment:

'How dare she swear at me!' or

'I need to get away from her.' or

'She looks upset, poor thing.'

Whichever thoughts seem real to you in that moment will give rise to your behaviour:

You might swear back.

You might walk away.

You might ask if she is OK.

You are not in control of the other driver.

You are not in control of your thoughts about her.

You are not in control of the behaviour that results from the thoughts.

You are not in control of any of it.

Does this mean you are an automaton?

Are you just an oblivious receiver and transmitter of whatever appears in your head?

You would be... but, fortunately, you have (or perhaps we should say 'are') consciousness.

Consciousness brings thought alive as though it were real. It also allows the realisation that thoughts are ever-changing, transient, neutral mental energy.

Inherent in this gift is 100% custody for what you believe in any moment. And 100% custody for what you do as a consequence of that belief, even though what you believe is out of your control.

Crazy isn't it?

Even though you have no control over the road woman, for the moment that she is in your life, she is in your care. Every single thing about her is perceived through your mind in that moment. She can't exist for you other than through your experience of her.

It is the same for all thoughts. You have no control over when and how and what will appear. Once these thoughts appear in your head, though, they are in your custody.

You have no choice about the behaviours that come from those thoughts. The behaviours though are in your custody. Only yours.

So there we have it: 100% custody of anything that appears within our awareness, 0% control.

Kahlil Gibran said, "Your children are not your children. They are the sons and daughters of Life's longing for itself. They come through you but not from you, And though they are with you yet they belong not to you".

It is the same for everything else in our lives.

You have custody of your thoughts because they are arising in your mind. They are not in your control.

You are the custodian of your mood because it is arising within you. Your mood is out of your control.

You have custody of your career/job/future because it is you that is experiencing it. Your career/job/future is out of your control.

You are the custodian of what you believe. What you believe and don't believe is not in your control.

You have custody of your behaviour. What you do and don't do, say or don't say is not in your control.

All of this is 'life's longing for itself. Coming through you but not from you'.

Custodianship of our experience without control. This is the truth of our existence.

We suffer because most of us believe the opposite.

We suffer because we believe that we *should* have control over our thoughts, our children, our behaviour, our future, our employees, our experience, our diet, our moods, our environment, our circumstances, our career, our mental state, our money, our confidence, our habits, our motivation.

We believe we should have 100% control or we are somehow lacking.

At the same time, we completely overlook the fact that all of this is an experience of thought in the moment. We forget that every perception, implication, meaning, feeling, opinion about any of it is being generated within awareness. And because we forget, we take 0% custodial responsibility for this experience.

This misunderstanding is the origin of every problem we ever have and every conflict in which we ever find ourselves.

When we live, believing the opposite of who we really are and where our experience comes from, we suffer.

But in understanding the nature of the mind, everything changes.

Knowing it is simply thought arising from moment to moment within us, we take 100% custodial responsibility as the space in which the experience of life, the experience of ourselves and the experience of everyone else is created.

Knowing that everything changes all the time, we realise we have 0% control over any of it – no control over what others think, say or do, no control over what will appear in our mind in the next five minutes, no control even over whether we will wake up in the morning.

The awareness of this truth glows out from the most inspiring leaders. These are the people who live in the realisation of ultimate custody of the world because it is a world within their awareness. At the same time, they are fully aware that no control of it is possible, that change is built into its nature.

These are the people who understand their role in the centre of the universe.

They know reality is being created moment by moment through thought.

They realise that the only way violence will ever end is when they are able to look with peace on the perpetrators of violence. The only way hatred will ever end is when they love the people who are hating. They notice ill-treatment and they look to their own lives for where they themselves are mistreating others.

They realise that when they hate those that hate or wish violence on those that commit violence or judge those that judge, they are proving to themselves the impossibility of acting differently from what they are thinking and believing in that moment. If they can't do it, how can they expect anyone else to?

To come to this truth of life, all we can ever do is to notice.

Notice.

Because in the noticing is the realisation of what we are bringing into existence in that moment: a man, a thought, a woman, a child, a mood, a circumstance, a past.

This is our custodial responsibility.

To notice.

To observe.

To become clear.

To see more.

To come time and time again into the truth of our experience.

And when we forget the truth, to be compassionate with ourselves and with others who also forget.

There is guidance that tells us when we are close to the truth. This is the deep feeling of realness, simplicity, love and connection.

This is the rudder that steadily draws us through an external reality which changes from moment to moment. There is nothing out there that we can use as a reference point. We can only use our deepest feeling of knowing.

You are the custodian of all of it.

YOU ARE NOT IN CONTROL.

YOU ARE NOT YOUR STRESS

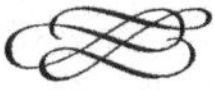

Nothing in life is as important as you think it is when you are thinking about it.
Daniel Kahneman

Our mental energy changes from one moment to the next. One moment it is high and we see solutions and possibility. The next moment it is low and we see people who are out to get us and situations that seem impossible.

We all experience this. Things that seem insurmountable at one moment, seem manageable in the next. Our spouse or children or colleagues can seem intolerable at one moment and the loves of our lives in the next. It is not situations and people that change from minute to minute, it is thought.

Our state of mind is not in our control. Which could be a problem if we felt we always needed to see solutions and possibility. But when we realise that our state of mind changes all the time, that what we see out there is no indication of reality, we can just let our mind do its thing and take it less seriously.

This is the end of stress.

It is the end of believing that we have to change anything we see 'out there' to be OK.

It is the end of believing that we have to feel a certain way in order to be OK.

Do you believe what you experience to be objective reality? It would be understandable if you do. It looks and feels real, after all!

In a low state of mind, it looks like there are problems to solve and awful people to avoid. In that low state of mind, our mind can thrash around trying to come up with a way to sort things out in order that we feel better. Piling on more anxious and confused thinking just prolongs the time in this low state of mind.

It doesn't help that many of us have been conditioned to believe that feelings of worry and concern mean that something needs more attention, not less. If it causes stress, then we believe it must be worth thinking and worrying about. Stress has come to mean valid, important and urgent. Stress looks like we are taking responsibility. The result, of course, is more stress.

What a breakthrough it can be to realise that in a low state of mind we can't easily see answers and also that there is nothing we need to do to try to fix that state of mind. High. Low. High. Low. High. Low. High. Low. This is simply the human experience.

When we take a low state of mind seriously, we are caught up in what we imagine and believe, in fear, anger, anxiety, hate. There are no solutions to these feelings however much we lose ourselves in trying to find them.

When we don't take that low state seriously, we let the roller coaster of mind take its course and soon we are back in touch with innate love, creativity, peace and connection. And when the roller coaster goes back down and for that moment we lose that sense of who we are, that is OK too.

You are not your stress.

Comparison is the death of joy.
Mark Twain

As a junior executive in a PR agency, I would go along to meetings with my boss and wonder what is the point of my being here?

I would think: she has 15 years more experience than me in this. She has run many more campaigns. She has dealt with hundreds more clients. She manages different issues every day. What could I say that will be of any comparable value?"

That felt very real to me. I didn't question it. And for most of the meetings, I sat there either in silence or agreeing.

Then fifteen years later I was a marketing director for a global brand. By then, I myself had run many campaigns and dealt with hundreds of issues. I was in a meeting with someone in her early twenties who had just joined our team.

I thought, "How great that we will have her perspective on this project. She lives in a different world to me. The people she knows, the trends and discoveries she is experiencing are so unique to her. The things that are important to her or not important are so different from my outlook. She will bring a lot to this discussion."

Then it hit me. Fifteen years ago I had had my own unique perspective. I had my own way of seeing the world, my own wisdom that would be relevant and useful.

I hadn't seen it at the time because I was too wrapped up in comparing myself. As a result, I opted out. I didn't even take part. In worrying about being less knowledgeable, less experienced, less respected I missed out. For no reason. Shame.

It is so natural to look out at what we see outside to work out how we are doing.

We compare ourselves to those who have reached the top of our profession. We compare ourselves to people we went to school with. We compare ourselves to people doing what we would love to do. We compare ourselves to people who are younger or older, to our siblings, friends, colleagues, bosses…

I still catch myself doing it now. I hear brilliant speakers and I think 'Will I ever be as articulate and eloquent and charismatic as them?" When I try to be like someone else, I am caught up in looking to a made up outside for information about what this made up self should be like.

When we compare ourselves to someone else we are only ever comparing a momentary idea of who we are with a momentary idea of who someone else is. Of course we can improve our ability in a particular area, we can always learn more and practice more. But to compare ourselves to anyone else is to completely miss the point of who we are.

CLARE DIMOND

You are not comparable

You are not comparable

YOU ARE NOT A VICTIM

Don't Take Anything Personally.
Nothing others do is because of you.
What others say and do is a projection of their own reality, their
own dream.
When you are immune to the opinions and actions of others, you
won't be the victim of needless suffering.
Don Miguel Ruiz

few people I know have been told by various institutions or counsellors that they are victims of abuse.

They have sought help because they are feeling scared and helpless. A well-meaning person, wanting to do the best for them provides a comforting label: victim.

'You are ' says the expert, 'a victim. You are a victim of your violent spouse or controlling partner or bullying boss.'

VICTIM.

It is a label that conjures up a frightening world of our mistreatment. It tells us there are people out to harm us.

It is given out with so much good intention.

You are vulnerable, susceptible, unsafe, at risk.

He or she is evil, nasty, manipulative, calculating, controlling, violent.

It would be helpful, this label, if it was truthful. But it isn't.

So it is unhelpful.

It is unhelpful because it prolongs the suffering of the person. It misses the opportunity to show him or her why they are not a victim of another person.

Anytime that we tell someone they are a victim we are reinforcing the misunderstanding that our thoughts and feelings tell us about how the world is. It tells us that how we are seeing ourselves and other people is correct.

It tells us that those feelings of helplessness are because we are helpless.

It tells us that we do not have the wherewithal to move away from people with whom it makes zero sense to stay.

It says 'yes yes yes' to our fear that the world is dangerous.

It tells us that our thoughts of dependency and weakness are true.

The truth is, though, that I am never a victim of a bullying boss. I am only ever believing powerful thinking that creates a monster in the office to tiptoe around and pacify at all costs.

I am never a victim of a financially abusive spouse. I am only ever experiencing a creative mind that conjures up a world and a limited self which has to depend on someone for money.

I am never a victim of a violent partner. I am only ever living a belief that tells me I need to keep someone who hits me in my life, perhaps even that I deserve to be hit.

In other words I am only ever experiencing thoughts and beliefs in the moment. And what are these thoughts and beliefs? Transient energy. Here one moment gone the next. There is nothing there. Nothing to even hold on to, let alone take seriously, let alone use as the blueprint for life.

* * *

LET'S look at it from the other side. The misunderstanding is also telling the boss that they need to succeed at all costs, that tension, pressure and shouting is a sign they are working hard and getting results.

It is telling the spouse that other people can cause blinding rage and that hitting out is the only option.

It is telling the financially controlling partner that her security depends on rigidly controlling money and people.

The whole circus is set up on quicksand. All of it is built on a total misunderstanding of what is really going on. This is the great illusion of our time. In looking to other people, circumstances or, indeed, ourselves, as the perceived cause of our suffering we miss the true origin of every problem, every act of violence, every feeling of helplessness.

Telling people, who are believing thoughts of helplessness and dependency or anger and violence, to take those thoughts seriously keeps them in the illusion. It points in the opposite direction of the truth that could lead to ultimate freedom.

Until we see the nature of thought, unconscious behaviour will meet unconscious behaviour and the two will escalate each other. The only possible outcome is more suffering.

There is no fault in any of this. None of us has a choice about what we are thinking or believing from moment to moment.

The boss is behaving in the only way that he or she can according to what he or she is thinking in the moment. The scared employee is acting in the only way possible given the boss her thoughts have created in that moment.

There is only unconscious, unaware behaviour, which is the reflex outlet of our thoughts or there is consciousness, an awareness of the transient nature of thought and action that emerges from a deeper, quieter, wiser place.

We have no control over whether we are unconscious or conscious from moment to moment. We have no control of our journey from one to the other. We have no say in our evolution towards clarity.

Blame makes no sense.

Blame is a nonsense word. It doesn't come into it.

When we don't see the truth of our experience, we have to put our energy into changing other people or the world in order that we can feel OK.

When we do see the truth, it is impossible to act in a way that contradicts innate well-being, creativity and resourcefulness.

What is the way out?

The single only way out for any of us is through realisation of the immense creative power of thought to create our feelings in the moment and of our innate guidance that will steer us, with integrity and clarity, towards what makes the most sense.

This is it. There is no other way.

Because anything else, any other well-meaning intervention or label or advice or strategy will point us towards a made-up world and a made-up self that has to change in order for us to be OK.

The on-going revolution in our understanding of mental health will mean that one day, every professional working in the care of others will point people towards the power of thought.

Not simply so that they can look together in amazement at individual reality.

Not simply so they can marvel at the human miracle and our incredible creative capacity.

But because in that realisation is access to every resource an individual will ever need.

Because in that realisation is the end of suffering.

It is the end of the perpetrator and it is the end of the victim. Neither can survive under the microscope.

When we truly see that we live in a reality created by thought in the moment, we have freedom. From this moment onwards, we act without resistance. We do what we know to do. We get a new job, take someone to court, find a shelter, ask for help, report a colleague, leave a marriage, offer a service, care for our children, make new friends, change country, take on responsibility…

We can do all of this without the illusion that we are a victim, without the illusion that we are separate from our experience of another.

We don't have power over the mental state of anyone else. No one else has power over us.

Our thoughts though, they have immense, ultimate, dictatorial, controlling, violent, terrifying, appeasing power.

Or they don't.

YOU ARE NOT A VICTIM.

YOU ARE NOT SEPARATE

*There's no separation between self and other, and everything is
interconnected.
Once you are aware of that you are no longer caught in the idea
that you are a separate entity.*
Thich Nhat Hanh

The definition of a vacuum is true empty space – an
environment with nothing in it.

It is the attempt to create a 'nothingness' within the all-
pervasive 'somethingness' of the universe.

Nothing cannot exist in nature because nature immediately
fills that nothing with something. Trying to separate out
creates a state so profoundly unstable that it immediately
disappears.

And this has profound implications for us and what we want.

Let's start with the fact that the separate human self is essentially a vacuum.

'That sounds a bit insulting Clare' you might say 'Are you calling me empty space? Are you saying I'm needy? Unstable? That I can't exist?'

Yes. I'm afraid so. That is what I'm saying. It's the same for me. It is the same for all of us.

When we try to separate ourself we create a state so empty, fragile, unstable and impossible that it has to immediately disappear.

The self cannot exist as a separate entity from what is being perceived because all of it is perception.

Any attempt to separate it is essentially the attempt to create a stable vacuum in nature.

Impossible. Doomed. The state of separation is so intolerable, so unachievable that it must obliterate itself.

When a vacuum is created in a laboratory it collapses instantly. Anything around it is pulled in because empty space cannot exist.

It is the same with a self that believes it is separate. Anything will be pulled in – pills, drugs, alcohol, sex, work, exercise, food, possessions, money, houses, people, approval – to make that intolerable, impossible idea of separation disappear.

NOW WHAT?

Well perhaps now we can consider that when we live from the idea of a separate self, our life is an attempt to do the impossible – stabilise and secure a vacuum.

We go in search of what we believe will distinguish us, separate us, give meaning to this separate self. Yet this separate self is by nature unachievable, it is inherently unstable, instantly collapsing.

Every idea of who we are is created from transient, ever-changing thought that appears and disappears. Everything we think about who we are can instantly, with a single thought, become opposite and be believed as just as true.

Like a vacuum, the nature of the separate self is instability. And this instability cannot allow itself.

Which brings us to the only distinction that ever makes a difference in our life:

Do you want what you want in order to stabilise the vacuum? To try to stabilise and secure a separate self? To numb the intolerable pain of believing yourself cut off from everything you perceive around you? Are you seeking love, money, health to create security, stability or to mark yourself out from others?

Or do you want what you want from the knowledge that you are everything already, that there is no separation, that you already have all the security, stability and love you could ever need? Is your wanting a celebration of life, connection? Do you know that it makes no difference to your well-being whether you get it or not?

It matters that we see this distinction.

One is a lifetime of unfulfilled searching and seeking, of insatiable needs and desires, of intolerable insecurity and instability that has to be numbed and obliterated with whatever means we have.

Every time we believe in that illusory separation, the imaginary void has to be filled and there is not enough money, drugs, alcohol, approval, food, cars, dates in the universe to ever do that because there is no void in the first place.

The other is instant, right now, in the moment peace. It is the utter relief from the quest. It is the sheer bliss of reality. It is the miracle of life expressing the miracle of life.

In our moments of clarity and absorption and merging and flow, there is no thought of separation, there is not even a hint of it.

We enter the arena and we are the field, the spectators, the ref, the ball.

We sit down to write and we are the unknown from where the ideas emerge, we are the keyboard, the words.

We get up to dance and we are the floor, the music, our partner.

We play with our child and we are the game, the laughter, the other small human in front of us.

We go to the shop and we are the money, the assistant, the goods we are buying.

From this place everything is possible. There is nothing to resist, there are no divisions, no beginning and no end.

There is no void to fill. There is nothing to secure or seek. There is no separation.

YOU ARE NOT SEPARATE.

YOU ARE NOT UP AGAINST 'REALITY'

We all live in our own thought-created reality. If we don't think something, it does not enter OUR reality. It doesn't matter if it's "there" or not; the only reality we can see and experience is the reality we create via our own thinking.
Sydney Banks

I coach from the principle that our reality is created from the inside out. That consciousness brings thought alive moment to moment and creates an idea of reality.

This means that experience is only ever a creation within the changing energy of mind.

And this theory completely falls apart the minute we consider our actual experience.

"Yes I get how it is all created from the inside but…

… my boss really is a bully, everyone agrees – even HR.

…. people are actually dying of starvation, that's not my thought.

…. my ex abused me. The police, my counsellor, the refuge – all said it.

…. I was mugged. This broken arm is not imaginary.

…. have a word with my doctor if you think I'm making up that I have cancer.

…. unless all the papers are lying – there are wars and terrorists and violence.

…. the bailiffs are banging on the door right now. I need money – real money – not bullshit about thought.

This is where a lot of people turn away from this understanding.

This is where coaches lose clients. This is where the coaches themselves no longer see how it can be true and go back to their old jobs. It is where the comments on an article or video post get angry and incredulous.

This is where it looks like denial or spiritual bypass. It looks like white-washing or fobbing off or head in the sky, skipping round with daisy chain necklaces la la la.

Because our ears, eyes, taste, smell, touch, memory that we have relied on our entire lives are saying, 'This is real'. Our experience is telling us: 'That really happened and this is really happening'.

And now someone is saying that the whole thing is an experience of thought. And not just that. Someone is saying that the whole entire thing is created within consciousness. That none of it exists – not the mugger, the bailiff, the boss, the cancer, the abusive ex – outside of our experience. How can that be?

Well if we stick around a bit longer we might concede 'maybe there is a tiny bit of truth in this'. We can see how other people create drama or problems or offence or anxiety out of thin air. We can find the reality that others think they live in incomprehensible. We can pity them for the things they think are frightening. We can be bemused by the things they think are important.

But the stuff that is going on in our lives? For us, that looks absolutely real. That does not look like a creation. It is just us reacting as any normal person would to the life we have.

And that's good. That means the design is working well.

Because that's why we're here, to experience life as if it were real.

The simplest, most fundamental point of life is to live it. Every time we get angry at politics or scared about a presentation or amazed by a sunset or turned on by our partner or happy about a compliment that's what we're doing. Living.

This experience of life is not possible without a self that experiences it and a body that senses it and a world and other people to create reactions.

And all of it (and, when we get real and quiet and simple, we know this to be profoundly true) is coming from within us. We know this because what is brought alive is unique to us. What is vivid or breathtaking or wounding or vital or irrelevant or obvious or not even present within our consciousness is ours alone. It is unique to us and unique to the moment in which it is experienced.

Then (if you are like me) you might say 'So you're saying that this scary world of terrorists and money worries and the shit boss and the health problems is my experience in consciousness. You are saying it is my projection. If that's the case, then how can I project more of the beach house and the sexy partner and the wildly successful business and great hair and world peace (in that order)?'

In other words: If it is all a projection then tell me how to stop projecting this crock of shit and project more pots of gold.

And this is where it gets interesting. This is where we realise that we are a double existence.

I am the person angry at her boss and I am the observer of anger.

I am terrified of public speaking and I am aware of the experience of fear.

I am devastated by a diagnosis and I am witnessing devastation.

I am the thought and I am the space in which the thought arises.

I am and I am the observer of I am.

Seeing even the slightest difference between the two makes all the difference.

The profound difference is in this shift:

From a self that needs a world and other people and its experience to be a certain way and which will do anything, hide, eat, inject, shop, lie, drink, work, fight, clean, save, compete, exercise, seduce, steal, help, whatever in the attempt to secure itself.

To an awareness of an experience of a self and a world and

an experience of that self perceiving, creating and doing within that world.

There are no words for how enormous this shift is.

And all of us, because we are human, have the potential in every moment for both. Neither is better or worse than the other. One is living the full technicolour experience of thought. The other is living the marvel and awe at the power of thought.

But if you are really fed up with the 'crock of shit' (and it is this fed-upness that often brings people to this understanding—like the hook the instructors used to have in swimming lessons in the 70s to fish us out when we'd had enough) then hang out more in the space in which experience unfolds.

Because in this space all thoughts are OK. All pain is OK. All fear is OK. All anger is OK. All loneliness, sadness, desperation, insecurity, poverty, illness, rejection is OK. Because all of it is transient and impermanent. All of it is experienced through thought. All of it will change. There is nothing to resist. All of it is safe. All of it can take place within consciousness. All of it is welcome.

All of it can be loved, because all of it is life.

And the love changes it all.

With the love and acceptance of our entire experience those thoughts that had been crying out for attention, that turned themselves into the glasses through which we saw the world, can settle down.

We spend less and less time replicating the 4 D reality of our thoughts and more and more in the awareness of the incredible creative power of thought and in the simple, unstoppable momentum of the body.

Actions which before had only ever been an attempt to secure an unsecurable self now become the physical expression of simple awareness. We might still hide, eat, inject, shop, lie, drink, work, fight, clean, save, compete, exercise, seduce, steal, help but it will be coming from the truest, simplest, most heartfelt, rock-solid, clearest place.

There is no separate world out there. There is no reality to fight or resist or conquer. There is just the grace of perception and creation.

YOU ARE NOT UP AGAINST 'REALITY'.

YOU ARE NOT YOURSELF

If you believe you are your story, your experiences,
your human frailties and flaws, your history, your personality, and
your feelings, it follows that you're being authentic when you share
these with others.
But what if you weren't any of those things?
Kimberley Hare, The He'Art of Thriving

My Facebook feed is always full of people promising to make me the best I can be—happier, wealthier, fitter, more attractive, more successful, more popular.

They are coming to the right place because a lot of the time I believe I need to be better and have more.

I have all the shelter, food, drink and wifi I need so, according to Maslow's infamous hierarchy of human needs, my focus is now 'self-actualisation': affirming my identity, asserting my self, making my mark on the world, celebrating my me-ness, being the best I can be.

And in that self-actualisation, so the adverts tell me, is all the security, self-worth, confidence and esteem I could ever wish for.

And it is one big fat lie. Or to be more charitable – one big fat misunderstanding.

It is a misunderstanding because the very nature of the self is lack, incompleteness, instability and falsity.

With devastating irony, the more we try to 'find ourselves', the more effort we put into 'being someone', the more we seek to satisfy our needs, the more lacking, incomplete, unstable and false it seems we become.

Because every single aspect of the self is transient, ever-changing, appearing and disappearing. Everything I think about myself is based in thought. Every belief about myself is simply thought believed in that moment.

Even my body which looks like who I am, that seems so solid, real and objective is changing before my eyes. Every label—ugliness or beauty, illness or health, pain or pleasure, disability or ability, flaw or perfection— is a creation of thought in the moment.

All of it conjured up by a state of mind that changes like the wind.

So this self that I believe I am is nothing but transient thought. And therefore this self is inherently unstable. It can change in the blink of an eye.

It is inherently false because a new thought that looks more true can always appear.

It is inherently lacking and incomplete because to exist it has to be observed as separate – believed to be independent of others, cut off from the moment.

Every time I consider my self I am looking at incompleteness, instability and falseness.

To try to feel better at the level of the self is to embark on a never-ending search for whatever I think I need to find security – approval, love, sex, food, promotions, money, beauty treatments, courses, qualifications, relationships, likes, upvotes, clients, income, purchases, admirers, employees… whatever.

It will never be enough.

Because however much of this I have there is always the potential for a thought of 'not enough'.

I could have more money than anyone else on earth and I can still wake up in a cold sweat thinking 'what if I lose it?'.

I could be adored by millions and still obsess over that one person who doesn't seem to adore me.

Qualifications and hundreds of letters after my name are no guarantee against the thought, 'I am stupid'.

And I can waste an entire lifetime, burn through all my relationships, spend every penny I earn, work and worry every hour, in trying to pin it down, trying to find peace by making this self of mine something it can never ever be – real, fixed, better, secure, worthy, valuable.

This is insanity. This is suffering. This is addiction. This is desperation. This is war and terrorism without even leaving the house. This is the ultimate vicious circle that is at the heart of every misery.

So what is the alternative? To give up? To collapse in a heap of nothingness, indifference and inertia?

Well the alternative is something quite amazing.

The alternative is the answer to everything we have been seeking.

And it comes with the pinnacle of the pyramid that Maslow eventually added that not many people are aware of:

SELF TRANSCENDENCE.

Moving beyond the idea of self, realising that there is more to us, more to life than this collection of thoughts and beliefs. The awareness that self-consciousness is a limit not a goal. The knowledge that we cannot possibly be what we think we are.

But we know this already. This is ancient information.

When we were fresh from the womb, eyes still closed and we moved our tiny, out of control body, towards our mother's voice, we knew this.

When we were three years old, leaping up to dance the second the music comes on, life sparkling in every twirl, we knew this.

When we looked up at the night sky or the inside of a rose or a yellow dawn or a butterfly wing and we caught our breath at the wonder and perfection, we knew this.

When we laughed until we cried with a friend, when we made love with our soul mate, when we comforted a child, when we loved with all our heart, we knew this.

When we wrote on a page or ran on a pitch or picked up an

instrument or spoke in a meeting and allowed life to flow through us from the deepest unknown and appear as a sentence, a goal, a melody or an idea, we knew this.

We knew this. We know this.

We were told, and we naively believed, that we would find peace, joy, security through self-consciousness, through being distinct from others, through resistance to what is, through acquisition, through trying to control and make better.

How wrong we were.

All we are is a channel for life to flow through, for ideas, magic, love. The only purpose of our self-consciousness is to allow us to realise this.

Freedom is the freedom of realising that everything we think about who we are is an illusion. It is the freedom of seeing that every requirement we have, every change we desire is obscuring the perfection of right now.

Joy is the joy of seeing that this limited, separated, needy self has only ever been a mirage. It is the sheer joy of no self-reference, of expansion, of light-ness and wonder.

Peace is knowing that everything, however apparently unpeaceful, is welcome. We are an experience of all of it whatever it is. The choppiness of the waves on the surface cannot affect the still depth of the ocean.

The only time we get a glimpse of who we are is when we realise we know nothing, may never know anything, about who we are.

And this no-self place of joy, freedom and peace never seeks joy, freedom or peace. There is no search or seeking because there is no self that needs anything to be different.

It is in our disappearance that we become enormous and substantial and magnificent.

In our no-self we are every person, every place, every idea.

YOU ARE NOT YOURSELF

YOU ARE NOT

Why are you unhappy?
Because 99.9 per cent of everything you think and everything you
do is for yourself
— and there isn't one.
Wei Wu Wei

Every time we realise something that we are not we get closer to the limitless freedom of who we are.

It is as though we are in a hot air balloon grounded by bags and cases and heavy luggage. We pick up one onerous suitcase of stuff and dump it over the side of the basket. Then another. Then another. The basket starts to strain at the ropes as it tries to take off. Then the last lump tipped over the side and the ropes are no longer strong enough to keep the balloon down.

We become lighter, less encumbered, more real, more present.

Everything we think we are is a story that lasts a split second or a lifetime.

Freedom for all of us is seeing the thought-created self. The end of all conflict lies in the realisation that we are not separate. The end of all suffering comes when we see what we are not.

YOU ARE NOT.

PART 2: YOU ARE

All we are is peace, love, and wisdom,
and the power to create the illusion that we are not.
Jack Pransky, Seduced by Consciousness

We are not all the things we think we are.

When we take away everything that changes on a dime, that shifts and slides, that flips back and forth, we take away the content of experience. We realise we can never be the 'what'. We aren't the object.

What remains?

The second half of this book explores who or what we really are.

YOU ARE AN IDEA OF SELF

We ourselves are not an illusory part of Reality;
rather are we Reality itself illusorily conceived.
Wei Wu Wei

*I*magine paradise.

Not the regular paradise of hammocks and sunsets and pina coladas.

A paradise way beyond that, a melting, merging energetic intensity, formless and fluid. Blissful as love. Eternal as infinity. Indefinable as space. The abundant, creative source. Real, permanent, constant and absolute.

Imagine that this paradise is you. It is all you know, all you have ever known. It is who you are, there is no part of it that is not you.

There is no place where you stop and something else begins. There is no other. It is all of you and you are all of it.

Paradise cannot know itself.

As an absolute with no relative or comparison, it cannot experience its perfection.

As the source of all creation, it cannot know its creative power.

As everything, the understanding of infinite abundance is inconceivable.

As nothing but love, it is impossible for it to ever experience love.

So paradise takes action. It moves from the formless into material form. Minerals, plants, animals, humans appear. Everything apparently created by those forms appears: diamonds, flowers, nests and shops…

You and I, both paradise, both arising from the same energy, come into form as separate human beings. We each take on the idea of 'I'.

The sole purpose of each 'I' is to get as close as possible to the truth that gave rise to the 'I'.

The 'I' uses its human experience to remember its spiritual nature. It lives in form with the gift of awareness to do just that.

The 'I' notices moments when it seems incapable or when it feels hatred or inadequacy or when it falls out of love. It notices that these moments seem to contradict everything it knows.

It notices moments of deepest love, soaring creativity, unbridled joy. It notices that these moments chime perfectly with what it knows to be true.

Like in the children's game of 'hotter, colder', the 'I' moves further away from or closer to its truth. Its feeling tells it in which direction it is moving. Closer to home or further away? More separate or more whole?

The 'I' has glimpses and realisations of its nature. In each glimpse is the clearest confirmation of its completeness, its potential, its love. And then, because the 'I' is still an 'I', this glimpse must be forgotten.

Sometimes the 'I' gets confused between what is real and what is not.

Sometimes the 'I' tries to use these glimpses into the magnificence of its spiritual nature to be a better, more successful 'I'. It tries to find itself by being more separate, more distinct, more individual.

But this is to have it all backwards.

Getting better at an illusion is still an illusion. It makes no sense to look in this direction.

What does make sense though is for the 'I' to use the material world to remember its spiritual nature.

The 'I' is the child on the beach with the castle-shaped bucket, sand as far as the eye can see.

The 'I' is a being designed to love and, would you look at that, along come 7 billion people, wanting to be loved.

The 'I' is peace at its very core and it finds itself in a world of war crying out for peace.

The point of 'I' is to realise it all. It is to use the gift of human form to realise unlimited creative potential. It is to use this apparently separate form to realise wholeness.

The 'I' balances between illusion and truth, truth and illusion. It lives out the paradox of being simultaneously both 'I' and 'not I'.

The 'I' knows that the secret to not being angry, insecure or scared is to know it is here to be angry, insecure or scared.

It sees that the secret to engagement is knowing there is nothing to engage in.

It experiences great relationships by realising that relationships are impossible within one being.

It wins when it realises that winning and losing are the same.

It knows that the secret to change is that nothing needs to change.

It looks through its human eyes, listens with its human ears, touches with its human hands. It sees the paradise of who it is reflected back in every sight, sound, texture.

It remembers it is only an idea of a self.

Forgets.

Remembers again.

YOU ARE AN IDEA OF SELF.

YOU ARE THE SPACE IN WHICH THOUGHT, FEELING AND EXPERIENCE OCCUR

Wealth is the ability to fully experience life
Henry David Thoreau

We queue up to scream on crazy fairground rides. We go to concerts to be moved to tears of laughter or joy. Some of us leap off the top of cliffs or ski down near vertical slopes. We sit for hours in cinemas for terror, horror, elation, tension. Some of us choose jobs in which we are surrounded by the most profound sadness and grief.

The whole kaleidoscope of emotion is possible.

In the talks I do, people often ask, "How can I change my life or myself so that I am only feeling good feelings - happiness, joy? That's what I want."

The answer is that no emotion is objectively good or bad, desirable or to be resisted.

Sometimes fear is something we really want and we will demand a refund if the horror film we have gone to see doesn't deliver. Sometimes fear is desperately not wanted. I have many clients who come to me because they want to get rid of their feeling of fear when public speaking. They see it as a terrible thing.

Fear is a physiology that we label fear. Our thoughts decide if these sensations in our physical body are to be welcomed or to squashed at all cost.

We can say the same of happiness. When my beloved grandmother died aged 97, I felt the deep sadness of losing her. There wasn't anything wrong with that experience. Grief at the loss of one of the most beautiful, kindest people from my life made absolute sense. I didn't want to be happy in that moment. I wouldn't have welcomed anyone trying to cheer me up or jolly me along.

As we realise that our entire experience is thought-generated, temporary and transient we fear it less. We don't have to protect ourselves from strong emotions because we know they are part of life. As a result, many people find they are on an even more extreme emotional rollercoaster than before. They can feel the emotions because they are now safe to do so. No numbing is required.

And as we see this more clearly, our sensitivity rises. As we come more and more into alignment with the loving, peaceful nature at our core, it jars us more when we think, say or do things that are not true to this.

What was unnoticeable in a daily life full of conflict, stress, exhaustion and confusion now flashes a bright warning light. Our benchmark has changed. We are in a new reality.

YOU ARE THE SPACE IN WHICH THOUGHT, FEELING AND EXPERIENCE OCCUR

YOU ARE CONSCIOUSNESS

Your life is unfolding naturally. Leave it be!
It does not need any help. Stay as neutral awareness.
Mooji

In my son's nursery, all the children lay on big sheets of paper. The teacher drew around them and cut out the shapes. Then the children painted in their clothes and faces. My son was proud of his painting and it did look quite like him with his brown hair, blue jeans and red t-shirt. We pinned it to the wall of the kitchen with the feet of the painting level with the floor so that it was his actual height.

For about two weeks after that, every time one of us would come into the kitchen we would get the shock of our life. Because there was Finn. Standing by the wall. As though he had been there for hours. Except it wasn't him, of course, it was the painting. I would come back from dropping him and sister off at school, open the door and actually shout out loud because there he was in the kitchen.

Eventually (and I'm slightly embarrassed by how long it took) I got used to the painting. I would see it as I came in and know that it wasn't Finn. There was no shock or momentary bewilderment. Finn is at school and this is a painting.

The other day I realised that we had had the painting up for over 6 months. Finn is now much taller. We probably won't take it down until we decorate the house because the truth is that we have actually stopped seeing the painting. It is so much a part of the wall that we don't even notice it. Every so often a friend who has come for a visit will say something about it and it will take me a while to register what she is talking about.

This is how consciousness works. Things seem real. They might seem real for years, decades. All the time that they seem real, there is reaction to them as if they are real.

And then something happens. We read something or we see something differently or we have new information and we start seeing the possibility that what we thought was real might not be.

The more we consider this possibility, the more obvious it becomes that what we had thought was real might not actually exist.

Then we see it so clearly that we can never again believe it is real. It has ceased to be.

We have the potential to have this shift of perception, this realisation of truth with every aspect of our lives and self because the nature of our being is awareness.

Consciousness brings alive our thoughts so that we live in the experience of what we are thinking from one moment to the next. It allows us to experience what we are experiencing.

The special effects department of consciousness makes it all seem so entirely real. How can it be a film when my boss is being such a bastard and making me feel so insecure? How can it be made up that I don't have any money and that I am terrified of losing my house?

Surely all of that is real? It feels so real and looks so real. These are facts.

Consciousness has a second gift. It is the ability to realise that we are not our thoughts. In other words, it is the ability to realise that the film we are watching is just a film and that aliens are not really taking over the world right now as we sit eating popcorn.

So it is with our life. It is the ability to realise to a greater or lesser extent that what we are seeing as real, all around us, is just a film. Everything is experience and all experience appears in consciousness.

Through consciousness, we see more and more clearly that there is a far bigger picture than the one we see right in front of us.

This happens all the time.

We think someone dislikes us because they are being so quiet. We start to wonder what is wrong with us. We start to dislike them for disliking us. Then we find out they were ill during that meeting and a whole new idea of that person and our self emerges.

We get called into the boss' office and we think we have done something wrong. We think of all the errors we have made over the last months and how we'll have to start looking for a new job. We start to feel defensive. We start to think of the reasons why the boss is not good. Then she tells us we are getting a pay raise for great work. The relationship with the boss, the company and with our own prospects flips in a matter of seconds.

Does that person like us or not, do we like them or not, illness or no illness? Are we good at our job, pay rise or no pay rise, is our boss good or not, do they want us in the company or not? Are we poor or rich? Trying to find the truth in that is to go round a rabbit warren of ever-changing opinions and situations.

As we pan out, as we get a wider perspective, everything shifts. And all we can do is to pan out further and further to get the widest perspective we possibly can.

As our awareness broadens, we see more. As we see more we realise that the truest part of our nature, the only truth ultimately, *is* that awareness. The content, the experience, the film changes all the time but the knowing, the awareness, the screen on which the film is projected does not change. It is permanent, ever-present.

You are Consciousness.

YOU ARE CREATION

Thinking is the enemy of creativity. It's self-conscious, and anything self-conscious is lousy. You can't try to do things. You simply must do things
Ray Bradbury

All day every day, we are the space in which creation takes place...

The creation of...

- an idea of who we are.
- an idea of how the world is.
- a belief of what is required to be loved and respected and wanted.
- an idea of others and their thoughts and opinions.
- the appearance of circumstances and situations
- the definitions of success and failure.
- meanings, assumptions and beliefs.

Creation.

What we see around us and how we regard ourselves rarely looks like a creation. It just looks like how things are. It looks like reality. It looks like something that none of us has a choice in. Just the way it is.

Yet all of those creations come from the power of thought. They are all thoughts believed in the moment to be true. In that moment of belief, they become our reality. And that reality creates certain options, certain ways to behave, certain expectations and requirements.

Reality comes entirely through the creative power of thought.

All it ever takes to change that reality is another thought, another insight, a different perspective.

This is the infinite creative process we can observe. A vivid, emotional, experience created out of thought in a split second. In the next second the entire experience dissolves and reappears as another.

We have no power over which thoughts come to mind. And we can't stop ourselves thinking the thoughts we think. Neither can we force ourselves not to believe the thoughts we believe.

So where is creative freedom? Why are we not doomed to live a reality created out of thoughts over which we have no control?

Because we can understand that we are creation itself. We can see that we are the space in which pure creative power creates. We notice its impersonal energy and its ebb and flow.

We become aware of the fact that we think and we become aware that the thinking is arbitrary. *What* we think becomes far less significant than the fact of thought itself. We simultaneously realise the enormous power of thoughts and their irrelevance. They create an entire life or they pass through like a cloud across the sky.

When we realise the arbitrary nature of thought, then what do we have? We have an inner knowledge. We have an idea. We have a feeling of 'that makes sense'. And now there is nothing in the way. There are no beliefs about our limits or what people will think of us or what success and failure mean that would stop us from simply doing what occurs to us to do. We play the game that we are here to play as cleanly, full-heartedly as we can.

This is the distinction that changes our lives.

We can act from what we know to do, from inspiration, and we can do this knowing that everything we think about what we are doing and why can change from moment to moment.

When we do this we are coming as close to the truth of ourselves and of our life as we possibly can. When these truths are brought into the world, in the unique way of each individual, they can be world changing. These can be the works of art that move people over centuries or the heartfelt messages of the world's greatest leaders that speak to the humanity of us all or the feats of human excellence seen on the athletic track or sports field.

Or we can believe the thoughts that tell us that we would fail or that people will laugh at us or that it is a waste of time. This is how many of us live our lives.

The more we listen to what makes sense and ignore what is made up, the more we expand out into the world, creating, connecting and acting from a place of truth. This is how we are designed to live.

And with each insight we have, each moment of increased clarity, the easier it becomes to hang out in this space of simply doing what we know to do and letting the rest take care of itself.

What happens as a result of our doing what we know to do is out of our control, anything we think about it anyway will change. We can act on our inspiration and move through the world accordingly, marvelling as we do so at the doors that open, the people that appear, the experiences that emerge.

The translation of formless creative power into magnificent works of towering genius is unlimited and awe-inspiring. Everything we love that was created by a human (including all other humans!) began first as an idea.

It is also this capacity for creative thought that produces every problem we will ever have and every feeling of fear, anxiety or anger we will ever experience.

Creative thought brings masterpieces into our world that are so inspiring, so beautiful that they move us to tears, to become peaceful, to love, to forgive.

Creative thought brings sufferings into our world that are so intolerable we can be driven to kill either ourselves or another in an attempt to escape them.

We are designed so that all of it is possible. As we see over and over again in the news and in our lives there is no safety catch on humans that make it impossible for us to kill, wound, damage, destroy, insult, bully ourselves or others. And our nature means that we create vibrant, detailed, crystal clear reasons why these acts are justified, necessary even.

This is the reality of who we are. Unlimited creative energy moving out into the world through human form with no restriction whatsoever on the creation whether in our head or in the world.

And what is created depends only on how clearly we understand the truth of this. Because with each glimmer of insight everything starts to change.

There is no understanding that is more important for us to grasp than this one. There is nothing more fundamental to the future of humankind or to the planet.

There are a few things in life that we shouldn't look directly at. A silverback gorilla or the solar eclipse perhaps.

But who we are? What is true? What we are capable of creating?

Look that right in the eye.

You are creation.

YOU ARE COMPLETE

When asked 'Why don't you teach people to pray?'
Buddha replied 'I don't teach people to pray, because their
prayers will harm them.
Right now, anything they ask for will be wrong. I teach them
how to become conscious.
Once they are conscious they are free to pray for anything.
But I can say one thing: anyone who is fully conscious has
nothing to ask for.
He has everything.'

*H*ave you thought recently how you don't need anything?

No me neither.

In fact, I need a LOT of things.

I need my health, for a start.

I need to be alive.

I need the people I love to be alive of course. I need them to love me and to tell me they love me.

I need my income. Well, actually, I need a bit more.

I need a job that I like.

I need this house that I live in.

I need my children to be healthy and not bullied.

I need the weather to be a bit warmer and less rainy than it is now.

I need clothes and food and drink.

I need to have friends and go out.

I need holidays.

I need approval and people to buy this book.

I need to feel safe and secure.

And all of that is true if I am simply what I seem to be – a real person with emotional and physical needs and desires that must be satisfied for me to be OK.

But what if that is not really who I am?

What if I am awareness of that person?

What if I am awareness of an ever-changing idea of self?

What if I am awareness that the experience of a body and what it needs comes and goes with thought, moment to moment.

What if I am awareness that everything in living experience is simply thought appearing and disappearing.

I am an idea of a human self that is by nature vulnerable,

insecure and unstable that believes it needs all sorts of things to make it secure and stable.

And I am pure awareness of that idea of self, pure awareness of what that self thinks it needs.

In quieter moments we know this. We see that our idea of who we are and what we need changes all the time. That there is nothing fixed or objectively real about it, that what we experience is a creation of mind.

When we forget that we have this gift of awareness, then it looks as though it all begins and ends with us, this self, right here. We spend our time trying to stabilise and secure ourselves by making sure our needs are met.

What we don't realise, when we only see half of the picture, is that the more time we spend trying to meet our needs in order to be less vulnerable, insecure and unstable, the more vulnerable, insecure and unstable the self becomes.

This is because needs are created in thought. The more time we spend hanging around in thought, the more real it looks, the more energised and imaginative it becomes, the more branches it can add to itself.

The creative power of thought is an enormous gift. This is what has led to the telephone, the iPad, sushi, handbags, pyjama bottoms (to name just the things on my table right now - admittedly, am slightly embarrassed about the pyjama bottoms).

You might well have your own table and own examples...).

So it's all well and good and brilliant this infinite creative force.

Until it comes to illusory needs created by an illusory self...

Because a need created in thought can never be permanently met.

My five year old loves asking me 'Is 7 zillion spillion the biggest number?' so that I can say 'No. Because there is always 7 zillion spillion and one'. 'Ha ha ha' he says rolling around. 'What about 54 pillion dillion….?'

It is the same with thought created need. There is always another thought to trump any solution we create in thought.

It goes like this:

I really need a house to be secure.

What if I lost my job?

I could get a council house.

What if there are none available?

I could live with family.

What if they didn't have space?

I could live in a hostel.

What if there were no beds?

I would ask a friend.

What if they said no.

I would end up on the pavement.

What if it snowed? What if people hit me? What if I died?

And on and on and on and on and on and on and on and on and on and on and on and on and on and on and on and on and on and on and on and on…

As Einstein said we can't solve a problem out of the mind that created that problem.

So in thinking about and trying to meet these needs of ours, we spend our lives in the worst nightmares that this infinitely creative, needy self can produce.

If we think we need to be living in a house to feel secure, then even while living in a house, the imagination is in a sleeping bag on the pavement.

If we think we need approval to feel OK then even when someone is saying 'I love you' we are finding clues in the tone and body language that indicate the opposite.

If we think we need food to be safe then even when we have just eaten and the cupboard is stuffed full we experience the hunger of going without.

If we think we need sunshine to be happy then on the brightest, longest day we are already in winter.

If we believe our life depends on someone we love being alive then, over and over again, we live their death.

In not seeing the nature of need more clearly we reject life.

We cannot experience the right-this-minute abundance of the things we think we need!

Totally bonkers isn't it?

And the interesting thing about this thought created experience of not having what we need is that it has ZERO to do with reality.

The film going through our head of what will happen if the need is not met is an utter fabrication. It is a film of desolation and desperation. Its purpose is to isolate, confirm our insecurity. It looks fixed, real, terrible.

This film is a collage of all imaginary horror.

It makes no allowance for the fact that experience is ever-changing.

It does not show the access we have at any time to awareness of where experience comes from.

It does not feature the ideas that always occur the moment we get in touch with reality.

It denies the constant inner resilience that we have had our entire life.

It has nothing to do with the simple, clear reality of life.

This self is made of thought. The needs of the self are made of thought. The horror film of the unmet need is made of thought.

All of it created out of thin air, changing, transient, unfixed, unstable, unresolvable.

When we get really quiet, we know this.

We see that this house we live in is created and perceived by thought. We see that anywhere we live is created in thought. We see that we can experience the bliss of utter abundance in a cardboard box and the terror of poverty in a 17 bed mansion.

And so we walk around the house and every detail is perfect and allowable. None of it contains the implication of loss. It is simply what it is experienced right now. It will come and go because it comes and goes in mind.

We see that experience of life is created in thought. We see that anything we make life mean will come and go. Experience of the body comes and goes. Fears about health are creations from moment to moment.

We realise that we, as an idea of self, don't need to be alive, that consciousness does not need us to be alive and, in seeing that, we live each moment more fully and truthfully than we could have ever imagined.

We see that whether the people we love are alive or not, they are always the creation of momentary thought. We see there is nothing to cling to. There is no rejection of life because it no longer contains death.

Experience of others is experience of self. We are one being noticing itself. Our eyes drink in their beauty. Our ears are open wide to the sound of their voice. We are safe to experience them exactly as they are.

True living is to allow it all. All of it. The crazy thoughts. The desperate needs. The longings and the insecurities and the horror films. This self that is so insecure and unstable. There is nothing to resist. It is all safe in simple awareness.

Deep within we know, have always known, that we need nothing.

YOU ARE COMPLETE.

YOU ARE UNSTOPPABLE

This is the real secret of life — to be completely engaged with what you are doing in the here and now. And instead of calling it work, realize it is play.
Alan Watts.

Sometimes, when we discern the nature of thought and consciousness, we seem to lose motivation.

This seems logical. Why would we do something that makes no sense for us? Why would we chase success when we see that the definition of success changes like the wind? Why would we try to impress people that we now realise are reflections of us.

This is the shift from the foreground of experience to the background of intelligence. In the foreground, we attempt to change our experience of other or self to feel better. In the background is simple awareness of love, security and well-being.

And sometimes as we move from foreground to background we find ourselves in limbo.

We are beginning to see through the old beliefs that used to drive us on. But we are not yet experiencing the limitless freedom of our true nature.

Have patience. That is coming.

It comes with realising there is nothing we need to do. We realise that there is nothing we need to do to feel better. We realise the illusory nature of the self itself. There is nothing for us to prove. Nothing to change.

At the same time, we realise that there is not a single reason why we would not do what makes sense for us to do. Life is a gift, laid out for us to experience. A multi-dimensional, full colour, all singing, all dancing, all changing gift.

We start to realise our absolute freedom to take part. We are in love with the whole show knowing it is just a show. Laughing, crying, fearless, terrified, angry, happy... this is our life. We are fully, whole body, mind, soul and spirit, *engaged*.

We realise we are not in control of what we do. Ideas, actions, creations emerge. We are unstoppable. Our motivation is beyond us and it is through the roof.

Let's take this book for example. I don't know where the idea to write it came from. I don't know where each word comes from. I don't know how I know that one word fits and another doesn't. It writes itself.

At a workshop, two renowned speakers and bestselling writers were asked how they defined 'being productive'. Michael Neill said, "Doing what I know to do." And George Pransky said, "Acting on my wisdom."

These ideas, this wisdom and this knowing do not come from striving, analysing or force. They come from waiting, watching, listening, being curious, making space. The quieter, more available we are, the more obvious the solution or the next step. There is nothing we can do to speed up the arrival of the insights or ideas and the harder we try the more disruptive we are.

We have an idea of something we want to create or do or bring to the world and we know it is just an idea. We know we can't control the outcome. We know it won't make us any more worthy or make people love us. We know it won't bring us security. We know it doesn't need to because we have all that already.

And, far from keeping us stuck in front of the TV, knowing this releases the brakes.

The force of the oceans, the energy of the tiger, the brilliance of Einstein, the stamina of the Masai, the lightness of the sunbeam are powering us. It is all there, coming out into the world through us, in the way that only we can do it, say it, create it.

There is nothing in the world to stop us going all out to bring the love that we are into this made up world of ours.

We are life's energy, force, might and pure dynamism.

YOU ARE UNSTOPPABLE.

YOU ARE INTELLIGENCE

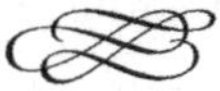

Joy in looking and comprehending is
nature's most beautiful gift.
Albert Einstein

*I*magine if we had to do everything ourselves. If we had to consciously digest our food, send the nutrients to the cells. Imagine if we had to create the seeds that give rise to the plants and the soil and water they use to grow.

Imagine if we had to work our lungs so that oxygen would reach the arteries. Imagine if we had to manufacture that oxygen.

Imagine if every time we had a cut or a cold we had to direct the immune cells to heal ourselves.

There is so little that we actually need to do. Yet we think in our lives we have to do it all.

For most of my life I thought that it was all on my shoulders and if I didn't strive and toil and manoeuvre and manipulate then either nothing would happen or I would fall into the abyss.

This is stressful. This is fighting to stay alive, struggling against the tide.

The world is laid out for us. There is oxygen and food and a body that knows how to breathe and digest. There is sunlight and lakes and mountains and rain and faces and animals. There are people to love and to talk to and there are ways to love them and talk to them or ways to be alone. There are words to write and the means to write them down. There is a voice and songs to sing.

We are the central point of an infinite intelligence. The breathtaking beauty of the rising and setting sun or the wonder of one animal helping another or the joy of a toddler learning to walk - all of it experienced through us. All of it brought alive within 'our' awareness.

When we feel very small or very isolated it can be quite a leap to see ourselves as powerful as the ocean waves or magnificent as the sun set in Hawaii or as intelligent as Einstein. But that power, magnificence and intelligence would not exist without the awareness that we make possible. The wonders of life are experienced in consciousness. Thanks to us. We bring them alive.

We are the infinite intelligence that powers and organises the world. The only thing that is stopping us from living in the knowledge of that is that we believe the thoughts that tell us otherwise.

We cannot fathom the intelligence that is powering our brain, that gives us awareness of ourselves and of a world around us. We know that we are intrinsically connected to everyone and everything yet that understanding of how and why is far beyond us.

If there is anything permanent or reliable about us at all, it is that we are the source of intelligence. We are the intelligence itself. And the intelligence uses the form of thought, appearing in the form of a body as the very first step in creation.

Through this human form, the intelligence that we are creates buildings, rage, elation, jealousy, paintings, businesses, music, arguments, conversation, mass shootings, hospitals, novels, dinner, bike rides, cruise ships, weapons, operas, wars, rock concerts…

This organising power is breathing and healing us. We are standing up, sitting down or lying down without even thinking about it. We are choosing tea or coffee or who to marry or where to work.

We cannot not be part of the intelligence. We are the intelligence.

YOU ARE INTELLIGENCE.

YOU ARE WELL-BEING

Life events can be tragic and challenging,
but who we are is never broken.
We have the resource of our true nature that does not exist in the
world of form. It cannot be comprehended by the intellect, but the
deeper knowing of the resilience and wellbeing it provides can
be felt.
Rohini Ross

I used to think that being psychologically well meant being calm or happy or in control of my thoughts and feelings.

This meant that I spent most of my life chasing peace of mind in course after course and book after book.

It didn't work. I was often not happy. I was often in a state of absolute terror at the thought of speaking in public or getting something wrong. I ruminated on all the stupid things I had said that day and all the ways I might have offended people.

What I see now is that 'psychological well-being' is funda-mental and far-reaching. It doesn't matter if we are happy or sad in any given moment, calm or fearful, sleeping like a baby or awake for hours.

If there is life and consciousness, then there is psychological well-being.

The only difference is that some of us (like me for years) don't realise it is there.

When we don't realise we have it, we spend our time trying to fix ourselves or fix our thoughts or fix the things in the world. This is futile and we can exhaust ourselves in the process.

It is in the thinking there is something wrong with us and the trying to fix it that we suffer.

We add in struggle and complexity to our mental life.

We label some thoughts as acceptable and some that we have to try to annihilate.

We add in thought about the future and the past that we see as fixed and true.

We add in a state that we expect of our mental life that is impossible to maintain.

On top of all this, we add in self-blame.

This suffering isn't pleasant. It can be deeply, deeply unpleas-ant. *But it doesn't affect our psychological well-being.*

How can this be?

THE SUFFERING IS CAUSED BY A MISUNDERSTANDING OF HOW OUR MIND WORKS.

THE SUFFERING IS NOT A SYMPTOM OF A DYSFUNCTIONAL MIND.

I suffer because I believe that I have to fix my feelings or my thoughts or I have to change the world to feel OK. *The suffering, therefore, comes from an innocent misunderstanding. It is not that there is something wrong with my mind or me or the world.*

Thoughts flow through, consciousness brings some of them alive while others go unnoticed. This creates a certain 'reality'.

The more clearly I see this, the less I suffer. But whether I am suffering or not, I am psychologically healthy.

We can *deepen our awareness* of our psychological well-being. We *cannot improve* our well-being as that is beyond improvement.

Our well-being is guaranteed by an intelligence way beyond our reach. It is a perfect system for experiencing life. There is nothing to change in it, there is only more to understand.

With more clarity, the suffering starts to wane.

When we see the fruitlessness of trying to correct our experience we can back off.

When we see that feelings come and go without our intervention, we can let them be.

When we see that our mind does great exactly as it is, then we can just allow it to get on with it.

We can notice the stream of thought and know it is just thought.

We can notice the feelings and know they are just feelings.

We can notice the fresh ideas and the intelligence prompting us and realise we have our own inner guide.

Even the most depressed, anxious or deluded people have moments of clarity. Even in utter confusion, they have moments of knowing that thought is not a reliable guide.

I have had several clients who came to me because they had thought about suicide. A conversation of 20 minutes about the power and irrelevancy of thought was enough for them to see.

YOU ARE WELL-BEING.

YOU ARE FREEDOM

*When God whispers, "What do you want to do today?" I don't say,
"A part of me wants to do X! But I know I really should..." When
God whispers, "What do you want to do?" I might just say, "I don't
know. Inspire me."*
Steve Chandler

I remember the first one very clearly. I was sitting
on the grass in the back garden of my house with
my best friend from school. It was awful. Retchingly, wretch-
edly awful. That smoke hitting the throat, the coughing, the
gasping for oxygen, the taste of ash. My lungs were loud and
clear: 'What the hell are you doing?' they screamed. 'Tar and
smoke and tobacco and nicotine...? Seriously? What
the hell...?'

I blocked out the physical protests and persevered with
determination and commitment (in the way I hadn't with
piano lessons or German) until I became a very competent
smoker. Go me.

Over weeks and months and years of consciously overriding what my body needed and wanted, I developed a tolerance for the toxin. I continued until tolerance became a 40 a day craving. This was now my normal.

In Jean-Paul Sartre's L'Etranger, the main character who has just left prison speaks of how we get used to anything. Leaving prison with all its hardships was hard. The deprivations and restrictions had become his way of life. Similarly, the character Brooks in Stephen King's Shawshank Redemption kills himself shortly after his release, believing he cannot live outside of what he knows.

Layer by layer, cigarette by cigarette, glass by glass, mindless distraction after another, belief by belief, fear by fear, we create and then hide away in these prisons of ours. And we label them 'normality'. This is how things are we tell ourselves. This is how the world is. This is who I am. This is what I need. I cannot survive outside this.

Our normality seems to be about what we tolerate, how much shit we can take. We up our dose to numb ourselves to the side effects of the dose. We seek comfort where we can find it. Preoccupied, confused, insane, we draw these illusions of what we need around us in the way someone might still seek the protection of the partner coming at her with the raised fist.

Then something happens.

We wake up.

We come into the reality of what we are doing or thinking or allowing and we see how impossible this supposed normality is in the light of who we really are.

It might be because our normal has suddenly become unthinkable. A dear friend told me that the beginning of the end of her morbid obesity was when the doctor told her the weight had created osteoarthritis.

It might be because we cannot allow what has become reality for ourselves to become reality for another. A woman who has suffered years of abuse may finally leave the day he hits her children.

It might be because we see where this normal of ours is leading. We might realise that ultimately there will never be enough alcohol or drugs in the cupboard to numb us to a life so out of sync with who we really are.

Or we might, as many of the clearest leaders and thinkers once did, simply wake up one morning to the truth that we are not who we thought we were, the world is not as it appeared to be, that our normality of desperation and resistance was simply because we temporarily forgot the loving, creative, excellence and freedom of our being.

This is the ultimate shift. It is the switching on of the floodlights to reveal reality in centre stage.

We look into the eye of the storm. We see that all that destruction and suffering in its approach and wake was only ever caused by a mind and body out of alignment with simple truth. We realise we do not need to retreat from and defend against what has never been there in the first place.

We see how tolerance with all its incumbent resistance, hatred and helplessness had kept us trapped in the language of the standstill and stand-off.

'I should be different.'

'You should be different.'

'They should be different.'

'This should be different.'

These words simply increased the gradient of the treadmill while we sweated and strained. Our eyes were fixed on the same continuous repeat film of insecurity and inadequacy.

As we look into the eye of the storm, we realise there is never anything to change or resist. There is only what is. The cigarettes and the alcohol and the food and the insults and the violence and the fists and the pain come down to the simplest barest mechanics: humans beings, confusion, misunderstanding, thought, wisdom, love.

There is nothing in any of that to resist or tolerate. There is nothing to change. It is the one blink of an eye moment of life we have. It is all we have and because it is all we have, it makes no sense not to love it, exactly as it is.

In love, there is no such thing as tolerance. There is just love. There is nothing to put up with or endure or suffer. Nothing has to change. And in that truth is the possibility of change.

We can love the cigarette. We can love the person shouting at us. We can love the food and drink. We can love the fears and the insecurities. We can love the prison. We can love the fumbling awkwardness of not knowing how the hell life works.

And the truth of that, will, as it always does, show you that you are, always have been, always will be, free.

You are freedom.

YOU ARE POTENTIAL

*I am the wisest man alive, for I know one thing, and that is that I
know nothing*
Socrates

Our entire reality is ever changing, created by the ebb and flow of thought. We are in constant movement.

We see that past, present and future are only ever an experience of thought in this moment right now. There is only ever this moment. This is all we ever have.

The perfection of this moment is self-evident. It is consciousness experiencing itself through human form. There is no greater miracle than right now, whatever is being experienced cannot be improved on.

Through the unfathomable mystery of awareness, a split-second creation arises from nothing. The perfection is mind-blowing.

At the same time, *this perfection does not exist.*

From macro to micro, every element is in transit. Energy continually shapeshifting from one form to another. Nothing to hold on to, to fix on, everything transforming itself. There is nothing but pure potential for something else.

We live the perfection by knowing that everything, by the time we experience it, has already become something else, that it was never there in the first place.

We live our potential by knowing that right now, this exact moment is all we have.

We are particle and wave. We are this moment right now, fixed in time and we are the motion that says to be fixed is an impossibility.

This is the player so present in the perfection of the right now, that the next seamless move is already emerging.

This is the writer so absorbed in the words that appear on the page that the future of the book is written into every line.

This is the friend listening with such simple love to another that time stands still and stretches out for all eternity.

This is the person living in the knowledge that their whole life consists of this moment alone, welcoming with fearless, open heart the destruction and obliteration of this moment.

We are not the experience, the thought, the something new, the apparent reality. We are always only the potential, the possibility.

Whatever experience we are in, we remain the potential for something else.

YOU ARE POTENTIAL

YOU ARE WAKING UP

Some people know they are dreaming when they are asleep. You must also know you are dreaming when you wake-up. When you know you are dreaming when you wake up, then you are really waking up.
Mooji

Philip Pullman said, 'the point of life is to bring about more consciousness'.

And Henry Miller said, 'the aim of life is to live, and to live means to be aware, joyously, drunkenly, serenely, divinely aware'.

Two other quotes take us a bit further: 'The point of life is, according to John Burnside, the poet, 'The shedding of illusions.' And, according to Oscar Wilde, 'To realise one's own nature perfectly'.

Which leads us to the questions: Who are we really? What is our true nature? What are the illusions for us to shed?

But we know this already.

We have all had those moments when we see our truth.

Perhaps when we gaze into the eyes of a newborn, or when we learnt how to walk, talk or ride a bike. Or when we see an elderly couple holding hands on the train. Or when we have done something that scared us. Or when we were so absorbed we almost stopped breathing. Or when we created something that seemed to come from nowhere. Or when we saw the sun set or experienced a masterpiece. The moments when we are in love with the world, in love with ourselves. When we are an awareness of the creative, loving miracle of life.

That's who we are.

And those moments when we are aware of it, we feel magnificent and humble, unique and connected, supernatural and natural, truthful and beyond truth, alive and larger than life. We know from the absolute rightness of this feeling that this is who we really are.

We also know from the ill-feeling in our body and mind when we are clinging to illusion. I'm worried. The world is harsh. He doesn't love me. I don't love her. I'm not enough. I'm flawed. I'm inadequate. I'm despicable. I am limited. I mess things up. My future is bleak.

All illusions. And we know they are because they feel so wrong. They sit so badly with us that everything feels out of joint.

The only thing that ever gets in the way of 'realising our own nature perfectly' are those 'illusions' created by what we are thinking and believing right now in this moment. We can let those go.

Who cares if we didn't remember this yesterday or whether we will remember it tomorrow.

All that matters is that we can be 'joyously, drunkenly, serenely, divinely' aware of who we are, right now.

YOU ARE WAKING UP.

YOU ARE TIMELESS

*The past gives you an identity and the future holds the promise of
salvation, of fulfilment in whatever form.
Both are illusions.*
Eckhart Tolle, The Power of Now

*O*nce a tea ceremony master unintentionally insulted a Samurai swordsman. The swordsman immediately challenged him to a duel the next day. The tea master was terrified. 'I am going to die,' he thought. His wife persuaded him to find someone who could help. He sought out an expert to teach him how to fight.

All through the night, the expert tried to instruct his pupil in the art of swordsmanship. The tea master couldn't get any of the motions right. At dawn, the sword expert gave up. 'You'll just have to approach the fight the way you approach your stupid tea ceremonies', he shouted.

The tea master said a sorrowful goodbye to his family. He knew he was going to die. Without any skills or experience in fighting, he had nothing. All he could do was approach the situation in the only way he knew how. The only way he knew how was to do what he did in his tea ceremonies.

He sat on the floor, closed his eyes and relaxed his entire body. With gentleness and power, he released himself to the entire experience. He noticed the emotions going through his body and allowed them to be. He saw the thoughts about what had happened and what could happen and allowed them to be.

And all the while, he sat still, open, present.

Then he was ready. He drew the unfamiliar heavy sword over his head and waited to die.

Five minutes past and nothing happened. Ten minutes, still nothing. He opened his eyes. The Samurai was in front of him on bended knees, sword on the ground beside him.

The tea master asked him in astonishment 'What are you doing?'. The Samurai said, 'Forgive me. If I had known you were such an expert swordsman I would never have challenged you to a duel'.

Until quite recently I was on a very clear, logical journey.

The point of school was to get to a good university. The point of a good degree was a good first job. The point of a good first job was a better second job. The point of the better second job was an even better third job. The point of a sequence of better jobs was to save enough for a good retirement and then... what...? [sound of brakes squealing as the whole thing comes to a screeching halt]... Uh oh.

I'd been living as though the point of living is to fix my gaze on the future until the curtain comes down.

If the point of this minute is to set myself up for a great next minute, I am living to die.

(A great next minute will never come because I am only ever living in this minute.)

Death cannot be the point of life.

The past is only ever created in this moment.

The future is only ever how we allow our imagination of a future to affect this moment.

There is no real previous moment. There is no real next moment. The only reality is right now.

The point of life has to exist in this moment.

You are this moment. Your thoughts about it can come and go. Your feelings about it can come and go. In stillness, presence and openness, we realise it.

YOU ARE TIMELESS.

YOU ARE IMPORTANT

Being in a minority, even in a minority of one, did not make you mad. There was truth and there was untruth, and if you clung to the truth even against the whole world, you were not mad.
George Orwell, 1984

*Y*ou are far less important in this whole thing than you think. You are also way more important than you could ever possibly imagine.

And the reasons why you are not important and the reasons why you are vitally important mean life can be a hell of a lot easier than it is right now.

When I saw the truth of these reasons, it was like an enormous backpack had been taken off my shoulders. I relaxed for the first time in years and, in that relaxation, life transformed.

Let me explain.

You are not important because, when it comes down to it, you don't exist - at least not in the way you think you do.

You are simply a channel between an infinite intelligence and the world. You are there for the ideas and fresh thinking and new thought to reach Planet Earth. Basically, you are a human hosepipe. Or a conveyor belt. Or maybe you'd like a more elegant metaphor? A diamond transporter perhaps?

That is it.

There is no job description. No target plan. You are here to receive and transmit. You can't affect the supply, format, content, frequency or timing of this inspiration. The ideas will be supplied to you in the perfect way at the perfect moment and all you need to do is create the space for them to appear and do with them whatever you are inspired to do.

That is it.

What a weight off the shoulders that is.

It really has nothing to do with you. You are not in control of all that. You can simply know that these ideas will be expansive and just right. They will blow your mind and take you to places you had never dreamed of. Because of these ideas, your life will be more than you would have ever thought possible.

But remember, you don't create the ideas. They come to you.

You are infinitely less important than you think.

But wait…

These ideas that are being supplied to you will be expressed by you in the magnificent, unique, unmatchable way that only you can express them.

No one else is you.

You are the perfect channel for these ideas. The only possible channel in fact. You are perfect.

You are **vital** to this whole process.

You are way more important than you could possibly imagine.

Without you, this perfect expression could not take place. And the great news is there is nothing you need to do here either.

Because the fact is you cannot not be you.

And the more you let go of the need to be anything in particular or anything different, the more astoundingly, sensationally you you are.

You listen to what comes to you with love and freedom.

You express it in the only way you can.

You change the world.

YOU ARE IMPORTANT.

YOU ARE UNLIMITED

We insist on being Someone, with a capital S. We get security from defining ourselves as worthless or worthy, superior or inferior. We waste precious time exaggerating or romanticizing or belittling ourselves with a complacent surety that yes, that's who we are. We mistake the openness of our being—the inherent wonder and surprise of each moment—for a solid, irrefutable self. Because of this misunderstanding, we suffer.
Pema Chödrön

WHEN I WAS ABOUT TEN, I had a joke book and in the book was this:

'How do I get down from an elephant?'

And the answer was:

'You don't. You get down from a duck'.

Bloody hell. That joke mystified me. I could not work it out. I asked my sister. It mystified her too. We read it over and over again, shaking our heads in bemusement. Neither of us had a clue. How could a question beginning, 'How do I...? be answered with 'You don't...'? How could a question about an elephant, be answered in relation to a duck? The question and the answer seemed completely unrelated. It just didn't make sense.

We asked our Mum. She gave a shrug to say 'I get it but it's not that funny' and replied as she always did, 'You'll work it out'.

We couldn't work it out though.

And gradually it slipped from our mind. Although, obviously, it was lurking there because.... About eight years later, my sister and I were in a department store in Cardiff buying stuff for my first year at university. She came up to me with wide eyes and a pillow and pointed in reverent silence to the label.

The label said 'Filling: 100% down from ducks'.

We looked at each other like the two protagonists at the end of an epic film as the credits roll up. The quest was over. We were free. Finally. What had eluded us, for almost a decade, was now ours.

How do you get down from an elephant?

You don't. You get down from a duck.

This joke has much in common with my coaching. (Not because my coaching is a joke, you understand. Indeed not!) But because every question we ever ask ourselves can only ever be answered with something that seems as though it is answering something else.

Essentially, every question is a 'How do I....?'.

How do I lose weight?

How do I have more motivation?

How do I earn more money?

How do I have more friends?

How do I find a partner?

How do I feel less angry / scared / insecure?

How do I become a better parent?

How do I get more clients?

How do I stop smoking?

How do I get down from an elephant?

There is no end to how we think we should change or what we think we need to be happy, successful, worthy, valuable. There is no end of elephants to get down from. There is no end to how much we can beat ourselves up for being stuck on top of an elephant with no idea how to get down.

And the magic answer to all of it…? The answer to all the 'How do I's…?'

You don't.

We could contemplate this 'you don't' for eternity and still not get close to seeing the magnitude of it. Here is where I am starting with it.

'You don't' because it is never you doing the doing.

It is not you doing the doing. The doing comes through you. None of that is in your control.

Just as we are being breathed, we are being eating, being drinking, being exercising, being watching tv, being running a marathon. We don't have any say in any of that. If we are doing it we are doing it. So we can move beyond wanting to change our behaviours, obsessing over better morning routines, stressing about being richer or more successful. We can just fully notice and accept and love exactly what it is we are doing. Because that is our most perfect expression of life right now. That is what we have.

Why waste a second of this precious time on earth in the desire to change a single thing? Any idea of what we are doing, any judgement of our action, is created out of thought in the moment. Are we exercising enough? Eating correctly? Earning the right amount? Talking to enough people? There's literally no answer to that which doesn't change in a heartbeat. It is impossible to put a value on how we are doing, no judgement will ever have any meaning.

We are being. All we can do is notice what is being done through us and love it. It's all we've got and it is magnificent.

You don't.

'You don't' because there is no 'you' to do anything.

Who is this you anyway? Who is this you that needs to improve or to stop doing stuff or do more of better stuff? Try and find it. What is it? Your personality? Your past? Your body? Your beliefs? Your behaviour? Your identity? It can't be any of this. All of this changes all of the time.

Are we rich or poor? Doing well or doing terribly? Popular or lonely? Angry or calm? Depressed or happy? All of the above. None of the above. We are all of it and none of it.

There is absolutely no possibility whatsoever that we are who we think we are.

So who is the one that wants to get down from the elephant?

There's no one there. There is an awareness of a wanting to get down. But there is no one wanting.

You don't.

'You don't' because there is nothing to do

Everything that we see around us is the creation of thought in the moment. There is nothing out there other than what appears through us. Anything that we think we have to do, is just thought creating an idea of a lack or a need or a should. As we see through this we realise there is simply experience of a body and a life.

There is nothing therefore to 'do'.

You don't.

Now what...?

The closer we get to the 'you don't', the closer we get to the truth of our lives.

There is nothing to do and there is no one to do it.

So now what? We turn into a little beam of light?

No, we turn into what we are, what we have been all along, a loving, infinite intelligence experiencing the sensational (in the literal and dramatic sense of the word) world of form.

With nothing to do and no one to do it, it is truly amazing what happens. We soften into the being done. Simply watching the loving force that moves the body, makes the speech, writes the words, kicks the ball, cooks the meal, drives the car, kisses the child, leads the meeting, takes the stand.

Suffering disappears. With no pride or identity, there is nothing to protect. There is no reason not to allow it all.

We are awareness of what is.

There is simply being, being without limit.

There is simply doing, doing without limit.

There is simply love, loving itself. No limit.

YOU ARE UNLIMITED

There is a vitality, a life force, an energy, a quickening, that is translated through you into action, and because there is only one of you in all time, this expression is unique.
Martha Graham

No one else can say something in the way that you say it.

No one else has your mannerisms, your stance, your accent, your vocabulary, your way of being present.

No one else looks like you. No one else has your way of looking at people.

No one else can move or be still, make sound or be silent, create or do nothing in the way that you can.

No one else can listen like you.

No one can write like you, sing like you, dance like you, paint like you, cook like you.

No one else has your insight or your intelligence or your thoughts or your way of putting things together.

No one else has your perspective, your take on the world.

No one else has your smile, your laugh, the expression in your eyes.

No one else remembers or forgets like you.

No one sleeps like you, wakes up like you.

No one cares like you, prepares like you, is aware like you.

No one else has your experiences, your examples, your way of telling a story or a joke or an observation.

No one else can love like you.

Any attempt to define yourself by any of these things will always miss the mark. Believing that any of this is who you are is to get lost in an illusion. Trying to preserve or improve on this uniqueness of presence is to clumsily melt the snowflake instead of gazing in awe at it.

I have a client who I speak to on the phone. I have never met her in person. I look forward to her calls in the way my children look forward to Christmas. What will it be this time? What joke or warm comment or beautiful insight or humble confession will I hear from her this week?

On one call we talked about how as we pay less attention to all the stuff that is whirring round in our minds, we become empty vessels, receiving and acting on the loving wisdom that is continually coming our way.

As we were talking, I knew that the principle was true. We are walking, talking, moving spaces. Yet equally fascinating to me was the form of my client that surrounds and shapes this space, the form that makes the shape possible. As we spoke, I knew without doubt that there is an essence of her, my client, that is indefinable and that is as magnificent as the space that we were discussing.

And it is the same for all of us. The same in the sense that we are not the same.

In focusing on the space within, we forget the vessel that is making it possible for the space to be. We forget that the vessel and the space are the same thing.

That is how it should be.

Because any thought of the separation sends us in the wrong direction.

'What are they thinking of me? How am I coming across? Am I getting what I want? I'm so different from them. Do I like this person? Do they like me?'

All of that is empty chatter. It just gets in the way.

Anything that we think about how and who we are and how and who someone else is is held in thought and has no truth to it. We cannot define it in words.

And yet... and yet... this person, this flower, this sunset, this creature is there. It is the unmatchable indefinable essence of each form. It is a miracle. It is unique. It is a work of art. It is exquisite, infinitely detailed, complex, profound. It is far beyond description.

To say that we are like the waves of an ocean, made of the same energy, appearing and disappearing makes sense. Yet in pointing to the sameness, we miss the indefinable, momentary glorious uniqueness of each of the waves.

Each wave is a shape through which the universe expresses

itself. And the shape is beautiful and beyond compare. The whole of life is held within that momentary form: the colours and the light and shade and the movement and textures.

As we realise that our idea of who we are is absolutely made up, the more this essence of who we are sparkles and dances and sets the world alight. The more intensely ourselves we become. The letting go of being just makes the being more mesmerising.

Even more miraculously specific, is that the wisdom that flows into the space that this being creates is designed expressly for that being.

Then the individual will shape it, express it, say it or turn that wisdom into a form that no one else on the planet could do.

Occasionally, the universal-turned-individual wisdom is fully, truthfully expressed, through someone's unique personal essence with so little separation in the way that it speaks to everyone.

The magnificence is such that the world catches its breath for a moment, takes a step back to hold onto a chair.

This is when the most profoundly moving timeless works of art are created; when humanity's greatest leaders speak words that end centuries of hatred and violence; when huge leaps are gained in medical and scientific knowledge.

And it is also present, in the tiny, numerous, every day unique expressions. When a parent turns a squabble over who gets the blue cup into a game for the whole family. Or when a nurse comforts a patient. Or when we decorate our house. Or laugh with our friends. Or become absorbed in our hobbies. Or work for a charity. Or write a letter. Or choose a new outfit or a new job or a country to live in.

All of us experience life in exactly the same way. All of us have a shape and a way of turning the formless into form that is impossible to replicate.

The more you realise that your idea of self is completely created from moment to moment, the more free you are to be the indefinable essence of yourself.

You are the perfect expression of life. The only possible expression in fact. You are perfect.

There is nothing to do here.

Because the fact is you cannot not be you and the fact is there is no 'you'.

No one else is you. You can never be defined or matched or copied.

You are unique.

YOU ARE LIFE REALISING ITSELF

Everything has beauty, but not everyone sees it. Confucius

...*A*nd the real wonder of it all is that for this unique essence, this miracle, to be experienced it needs a witness. Without consciousness, without awareness, it is not there.

In all this unique perfection there is nothing fixed or permanent or real. There is nothing that is independent of the perceiver.

In your experience, you bring me alive. Thanks to you, I exist.

In my experience, I bring you alive. Thanks to me, you exist.

When we see the pure essence of another, when we are free of any agenda other than to simply marvel at the unique being before us, we are seeing, in that beautiful distinction from ourselves, ourselves.

In that one exquisite moment, we witness the infinite kaleidoscopic gift of life and we know that is who we are.

We are consciousness realising consciousness.

You are uniqueness noticing uniqueness.

YOU ARE LIFE REALISING ITSELF.

YOU ARE LOVE

Your task is not to seek for love, but merely to seek and find all the
barriers within yourself that you have built against it.
Rumi.

Seeking love keeps you from the awareness that you already have it
– that you are it.
Byron Katie

Any feeling, emotion, judgement, idea, concept or theory that comes
from your ability to think (given that it's subject to change) is not
true. Love is the only thing that doesn't come from your ability
to think.
Love is the only thing that's true.
Garret Kramer

When we look for love or try to inspire it in others, we play all sorts of games.

We might try to become what we think someone wants.

We might play hard to get or wear our hearts on our sleeves.

We might try to be more like him or her. We might stop doing the things we love to do.

We might try to get the other person to change.

We might try whining, crying, shouting, needling, begging, cajoling, tantrums, gifts, tricks, new clothes, sulking, manipulating, bribery… ad infinitum.

And nothing seems to work. It always looks like there is something missing, that this love is not quite secure.

This is because we are searching in the wrong place.

How about going on an adventure to the place where there is nothing but love?

Let me tell you about this adventure.

Firstly, you distinguish between what is permanent and what is transient.

As you explore this distinction you realise that all experience of yourself and other people changes constantly.

With this insight, the belief in a fixed objective self and fixed objective others starts to lose its power. The idea of attaching your well-being and security to something that changes all the time no longer makes sense.

Awareness expands.

You realise that this other person is created in experience through thoughts and beliefs. And when these disappear, what is left? An apparent form that seems to have its own unique indefinable essence, a miracle just as you are a miracle.

There is simple, profound love for how life expresses itself in the creation of another human being.

Any thoughts about what you need from other people in order to be happy or how they must be in order for you to love them start to seem ridiculous.

You are in love already. You want nothing from anyone.

You walk around in love with the world and with everyone in your life. You know that everything is brought alive in the consciousness of which you are part.

Then your thoughts tell you otherwise. Your thoughts tell you that you need to do something to secure love. They tell you to worry about losing it.

Because the loving, connected state is becoming so natural, blissful and easy for you, there is no desire in you to entertain those thoughts. They pass through quickly.

Then you have a shocking insight – you realise suddenly that it is exactly the same for everyone else. The only thing stopping other people from living in this same deep love of life is what they are thinking and believing from moment to moment. Just as you experience, on and off, day in day out, in yourself.

You realise that underneath the mental chatter, they, just like you, are pure unconditional love.

They love you, they can't not love you. They just don't yet live from that knowledge all the time or even some of the time. Because you don't need anything from them, you can bask in the knowledge of that love without wanting to change what they think about you in any way.

And so there you are. Deeply in love with the people you are with. Loving and appreciating them exactly as they appear to you.

With you, they realise their simple perfection. They feel this in the depths of their being. You are the safest, most beautiful space for them because you are them, you are love.

There is no possibility they could not be in love with you.

127

YOU ARE LOVE.

YOU ARE PERFECT

*To me, every hour of the day and night
is an unspeakably perfect miracle.*
Walt Whitman

Here is a paradox. The understanding of our perfection and the giving up of the need to change a single thing is the rock-solid foundation of lasting change.

Our lives don't change by thinking we should be different and going out to force ourselves to change. Things might change temporarily on the surface. Underneath, though, the level of understanding that was creating that individual reality, and therefore that behaviour, remains the same.

Thinking we *should* change or that we *should* be different is the crash diet that puts on the pounds. The New Year's resolution that ends mid-January with a sigh of self-disgust. The chanting an 'I am a millionaire' affirmation into the bathroom mirror while our annual salary is going down the plug hole. The sorting out bad relationships by cutting off family members. The hundred push-ups on day one and zero on day two.

This is brittle, vitreous change driven by insecure thinking and misunderstanding which creates more insecure thinking and more unrest.

True lasting change occurs through a greater understanding of what our lives really are, of what they mean, of what is truthful in them. Because, through that understanding, we become different people living in a different reality. And, as a different person in that different reality, we will have a different resolve about what to do and different ideas to help us do it.

We become a different person with a different reality... It sounds dramatic but there is no other way to describe it. The slightest change in our perspective affects what we notice, how we react, what we know about ourselves and others, what is important or irrelevant. A fraction degree change in the course of an ocean liner sets it towards an entirely different country. A fraction degree change in our understanding leads to an entirely different life, to a different way of being, to different relationships and different resolve.

AND ALL OF IT IS PERFECT.

Whether I am this person, in this reality with this wisdom or that person in that reality with that wisdom doesn't make the slightest bit of difference. It is impossible for me to see beyond where I am right now because that involves looking at the world through eyes that I have not yet acquired, with a perspective that is not yet available to me.

In other words, I cannot acquire resolve to do something that I don't yet have resolve to do. I cannot change something that doesn't, with my current understanding of who I am and how the world is, make sense for me to change.

So all I have is right now.

And I can't change this 'right now' because change will come when I see things differently and I don't yet. If this 'right now' is all I have then it is everything. And because it is everything I have, because it is the current truth of me and because I cannot change it, it has to be perfect, right now.

So there are only two things I can do in any one moment:

1 Look for the perfection

This moment of saying goodbye is the last time I see them as they are right now. The blossom of this Spring will never be seen again. This moment is the only moment which I will experience as I am right now. Our lives are over in the blink of an eye and they are made up of single moments of never to be repeated, perfection.

Each moment is a perfect gift. Our idea of self is a perfect gift. The only thing that stops us seeing it is that we believe things should be different, that we should be different.

So where is the perfection in the pain, the heartbreak, the grief, the shouting match, the redundancy, the bill that sends us over the edge, the car crash, the diagnosis, the divorce, the rejection?

The perfection is there. With 100% certainty, it is there. And this has nothing to do with positive thinking or putting on a brave face or pretending. It is about tuning our ears to hear the indistinct and inarticulate whisper of love in our ear while we are shouting in anger. It is about gazing at the disaster scene and realising that in the periphery there is a blur of people running towards it to help. It is about sensing that if we allowed our armour to soften we would notice the hand in ours.

Because by extending the range and depth of what we notice, we extend the range and depth of our reality. When the Hubble operators controversially allowed the telescope to stare for 10 days at a seemingly empty sliver of sky, the resulting images of never-before-seen galaxies rocked the world. There is always more there. Whatever we see is fixed in place by our state of mind. Indeed, it is only there *because* of our state of mind. It is just one thing in an infinite landscape of things that we could also notice.

To see things differently is to realise a different person. As a different person, we will do things differently. For now, it is enough to know that if we are not seeing the perfection, it is because there is more to see. Our own personal infinite star systems are there, however blank the sky.

2. Listen for the calling

The reason the moment is perfect is because we receive wisdom designed exactly for that moment, given our current understanding or consciousness. Cathy Casey, a training consultant who has worked with prisoners and with teenage gangs, talks of the 'street wisdom' that can keep them safe in even the most dangerous situations.

The wisdom we receive is designed for us *right now*, with our weight, our health, our income, our relationships, in this house, with these pressures, in this situation, all exactly as they are right now.

In any given moment there will be a calling that relates exactly to this moment. There will be an obviousness of what is required. It might be to sleep, to make the phone call, to listen, to do nothing, to work, to walk, to run, to eat, to drink, to cry, to shout, to cook, to plan a holiday, to open a retirement account, to write, to practice, to strike for goal, to teach the class, to resign, to make love, to do twenty star jumps…

Whatever it is, it is there, for the life we have right now, unique to us. The calling is designed to allow us to move in the direction of the realisation of our true nature and true potential. *It is change by nature.* It is change without any apparent change. It is the already perfect becoming new perfect.

It is designed to keep us alive, conscious, aware, with a working body-vehicle expanding towards the realisation of who we are and what we are capable of and how much amazement we can have while doing it. The calling of each moment is so obvious that most of the time we just follow it without a second thought.

Then sometimes, our mind dips, we feel insecure, we start to question and we do have a second thought. We consider resisting the calling, we try to second guess it, we think we have to put something else in its place. But the calling is obvious for a reason.

******

Seeing our perfection and acting on the calling, we move through the layers of understanding. The obstacles and pain become tiny amid the abundance of everything else that is clearly apparent. The noise of our insecure thinking begins to sound harsh and discordant as the wisdom of each moment becomes more resonant and perfectly pitched.

YOU ARE PERFECT.

CONCLUSION

"To thine own self be true"

It's a famous quote from Hamlet.

People have it tattooed on every conceivable part of their bodies. It's on instagram, pinterest, facebook posts every day. It's stamped on planks of wood and hung on walls all over the world.

It can be taken as meaning 'Speak your mind. Stand up for what you believe. Say what you think. Act on your feelings.'

And, as such, it risks taking us deeper into a misunderstanding of who we are.

Shakespeare did not intend us to take those words as the solemn maxim they have become. They are spoken in Hamlet by Polonius who was depicted as a wordy and self-absorbed fool. The entire speech in which these words are delivered is meant to be ridiculous – humorous relief from the intensity of the drama.

And the maxim is ridiculous because this idea of self, of who we are changes all the time. What we believe changes. What we think changes. What we feel changes. What we want and value changes.

Everything that we believe about the self and everything we believe about the world can change in seconds according to the state of mind in which we find ourselves.

Being true to all of this is like being true to a cloud pattern in the sky or a configuration of waves on the sea. One second it is there, the next, it has turned into something else altogether.

It is 'I think therefore I am my thinking'.

And it pins us in the biggest illusion of our life. It keeps us trapped, looking outwards from a self to a world as though this self and this world are fixed, static and independent of our perception.

But if we look at that phrase again, if we use it as the prompt to sincerely ask ourselves 'who am I really?' 'what is this self to be true to?' it can take us to a level of understanding and insight that changes our existence forever.

Pythagoras said, 'Know thyself. Then thou shalt know the universe and God'.

Our idea of self, our idea of the world can only ever exist in our mind. We can only experience self or other through the power of thought and consciousness. We can only know the universe in exactly the same way.

Who is it then that is doing this thinking? Who is having this experience? We are something other. We are the awareness of thought and experience.

'I am aware that I think, therefore I cannot be my thoughts'.

As we come to the truth of our experience, we come to the truth of everything, because all of it exists through us.

And the strange thing is that the more we come to see that we have absolutely no idea who this self is, the more we seem to know when our life aligns deep down with who we really are. This alignment comes with a profound inner sense of truth and rightness. We know when we are being true to ourselves and we know from the stress, tension and unease when we are not.

This is the end of lying in order to reinforce our idea of who we are or to come across well to others. It is the end of manipulation. It is the end of pretence and exaggeration. It is the end of doing or saying anything out of a belief in a separate world and a separate self.

Instead, our actions and words come from the deepest, truest place inside us.

We have less and less tolerance for anything that is false or restricted or isolating. It jars with the freedom, love and integrity that deep down we know ourselves to be.

Moving into the truth of who we are and seeing more clearly who we are not, we become supremely comfortable with the discomfort of insecurity. We know that it will change from one minute to the next, that it has no bearing or relevance to us whatsoever.

As we realise our unlimited potential to create anything – any self, any world, any universe, we simply cannot entertain our old limited views that try to tell us what we can and can't do. In this expanded, boundary-less existence the path for us to follow is lit up like a runway.

What we believe about ourselves and the world becomes nothing more than a reason to wonder at a mind that sees obstacles and fault in one moment and opportunity and excellence in the next.

We discard the armour that we had long thought was necessary to protect and defend ourselves, and we become who we were born to be. We relax into our truth.

In the beautiful words of Marianne Williamson, 'As we let our own lights shine, we unconsciously give other people permission to do the same. As we are liberated from our own fear, our presence automatically liberates others'.

As we move into the truth of who we are, we realise that everyone in our lives is a reflection of who we are. How much we love others is simply the mirror of how clearly we see that we are love itself. Any disconnect with others is revealed for the intolerable disconnect with our true nature that it really is.

So the maxim, 'To thine own self be true', can take us in two opposite directions. Same words. Same tattoo. Same decorative plank of wood on the wall. Two entirely different lives.

One takes us ever-deeper into the illusion, stuck in an invented version of self that is insubstantial, untruthful and, ultimately, hard work.

The other takes us into the truth of who we are.

Constancy, freedom, love and limitless creativity.

This is the inside-out guide to being yourself.

A FINAL NOTE

In the final relaxation of almost every yoga class I teach, I say to my students something along these lines, 'Allow your awareness to go beneath your ever-changing thoughts and beliefs about who you are. Allow it to rest in the truth deep inside. The truth of love, wholeness, life, creativity, freedom, excellence and unlimited potential.'

I whisper to my children when I tuck them into bed, 'You are beautiful inside and out. You are everything you need'.

Mine is one small voice but it is now one voice of many all over the world, helping us all wake up to the fact that we are not who we think we are.

You might not be in my yoga class and I might not be tucking you into bed (you're probably quite glad about that), but please allow me to say the same to you.

You are love, wholeness, life, creativity, freedom, excellence and unlimited potential.

You are beautiful inside and out. You have everything you need. You are more than you could ever dream of.

YOU ARE.

REAL

THE INSIDE-OUT GUIDE TO BEING YOURSELF

BY

CLARE DIMOND

FOREWORD BY
GARRET KRAMER
AUTHOR OF *STILLPOWER* AND *THE PATH OF NO RESISTANCE*

ACKNOWLEDGMENTS

This book is in honour of everyone who has woken up to who they are and who helps others to do the same.

In particular it is written with sincere thanks to those who have helped me, either in person or through their talks and writings, to see this more deeply:

Francesca and Finn Dimond-Smith, Bridgit Dimond, Rebecca Dimond, James Smith, Bette Griffiths, Syd Banks, Garret Kramer, Michael Neill, Jamie Smart, Steve Hardison, Steve Chandler, Byron Katie, Amy Johnson, Kimberley Hare, Lise Dandanell, Mara Olsen, Aaron Turner, Lila Turner, George Pransky, Linda Pransky, Jack Pransky, Barbara Patterson, Rohini Ross, Angus Ross, Jason Berv, Phil Hathaway, Bill Pettit, Rani Bora, Nick Bottini, Nicola Bird, Terry Rubenstein, Peter Wilson, Jane Cockerell, Sam Jarmen, Wendi Saggese, Elsie Spittle, Cathy Casey, Jill Whalen, Mary Schiller, Dicken Bettinger, Ken Manning, Chantal Burns, Amir Karkouti, Grayson Hart, Adam Ashe, Ali Scott, Joel Drazner, Amanda Jones, Rebecca Perkins, Dave Kibby, David Westerman, Antti Vanhanen, Grace Kelly, Ian Watson,

Damian Mark Smyth, Elizabeth Lovius, Ankush K Jain, Jacquie Moses, Cherie Ray, Kimberley Kaase, Neeta O'Keeffe, Jean Lemmey, Claire Shutes, Mooji, Pema Chödrön, Eckhart Tolle and Rupert Spira.

Thank you.

ABOUT THE AUTHOR

Clare Dimond works with individuals, schools, businesses and organisations exploring how excellence, freedom, love and creativity are our natural state.

For materials, resources and programmes visit www.claredimond.com

Made in the USA
Monee, IL
28 January 2022

90133574R00100